W9-AAZ-965

Women Talk About
HOW TO GET MEN
TO TAKE YOU SERIOUSLY
In Business and In Life

By Linda Brakeall

HAWTHORNE PRESS
BOOKS FOR PROFESSIONAL WOMEN

Women Talk About
HOW TO GET MEN TO TAKE YOU SERIOUSLY
In Business and In Life
By Linda Brakeall

If you wish additional copies of this book, please contact:

Hawthorne Press
11 Arrow Wood, Suite 2D
Hawthorn Woods, IL 60047
847-540-0445
Linda@TheRespectedWoman.com

All rights reserved. No part of this book may be reproduced or transmitted in any form or by any means, electronic or mechanical, including photo-copying, recording or by any information storage or retrieval system, without written permission from the author, except for the inclusion of brief quotations in a review. No liabilities assumed for use of the information within. (C) 2003 by Linda Brakeall.

Manufactured in United States of America.

Library of Congress Cataloging
In Publication Data
Brakeall, Linda
Women Talk About
How To Get Men To Take You Seriously
In Business and In Life
Linda Brakeall
Hawthorne Woods, Illinois
Hawthorne Press, 2003

ISBN 0-9710209 –1-4 (pbk)
1.Success in business – Handbooks, manuals
2. Businesswomen -Handbooks, manuals

650.1/082-dc21   CIP

Attention colleges, universities, corporations, and businesses seeking gifts for clients: Discounts are available on bulk purchases (10+) of this book for educational training purposes, fund-raising, or gift giving. Special books, booklets, or book excerpts can also be created to fit your specific needs.
Contact: Marketing Department, Hawthorne Press,
11 Arrow Wood Drive, Suite 2D
Hawthorn Woods, IL 60047
8 0 0 - 6 6 2 -7 2 4 8.

Dedication and Acknowledgements

This book is dedicated to Tom Brakeall, to whom I have been delightfully married since I was 19, who brings me food when I have deadlines, does the initial proof-reading of my manuscripts, cherishes my body, eases my mind, soothes my soul and is my biggest fan!

...and did I mention he brings me food?

To Errol Smith of JackStreet.com, who not only came up with the title, but he was always there as sounding board, a marketing guru and a cheerleader.

To Marilyn Sprague-Smith who urged me on when I was tired, offered amazing insights and shared her wonderful friends with me.

To Brett Butler, who was the first celebrity to say yes, because, she said, "This needs to be discussed!" Please don't tell her manager she did this or she will be in big trouble.

To Cokie Roberts, who despite of challenges of health and schedule said yes, and was warm, funny, wise and unfailingly helpful and gracious.

To all of the wise women who made time to answer my questions, share their lives and laugh with me. It was an experience that I will always treasure!

Besides the noble art
of getting things done,
there is the noble art
of leaving things undone.

The wisdom of life
consists in the elimination
of nonessentials.
- Lin Yutang

Table of Contents

The first thing I do in the morning
is brush my teeth
and sharpen my tongue.
--Dorothy Parker

Production Notes:

I'm sure someone else could have done better job editing this book than I did, but I felt such a kinship with these women that I was unwilling to hand it over to anyone else. As I read, re-read and edited each interview I smiled and I cried. I cried at the courage in the face of adversity, the braving of the unknown, and heroic efforts -- often without support. I smiled at the wit, the love, the wisdom, and the generosity of each and every one of these women. So I apologize in advance for errors of commission or omission.

You will notice that the biographical and professional information is in a variety of formats. That is because I printed it very much as I received it, was only minimal editing. This is their story and I wanted them to tell you in their way.

The creation of this book is a tribute to woman-power. Women dropped everything to help me get this done in time. Women shared their time and their friends with me. As I was doing the first few interviews, I cautiously asked if it would be okay if I sent the transcripts to the interviewee for review. I was merely trying to compensate for my newly developing interviewing skills. I was looking for reassurance. The first two agreed immediately and the third said, *"What a respectful thing to do! I've given many interviews and had no idea what was going to be printed until it was published. This is just wonderful."*

As I thought about her remarks I understood fully what she was saying. I, too, am interviewed all the time. Many times what I have said to reporters had little or no resemblance to what was printed. Together, we have created a new way of doing this.

Instructions for using this book:

1. Create your own personal index on the inside back cover. List the page and topics that speak to you as you read.

2. Make a list of all the things that you want to incorporate into your own life. On page 201, you'll find several pages for your own notes. Right *here* where you can't lose them!

3. Prioritize that list. Which **single thing** would have the greatest impact on the rest of your life? Do that first. Then choose No. 2 and so on. You may not get through your entire list but if you do **the first thing first**, progress is inevitable.

4. Teach other women what you've learned.

5. Let me know how you're doing! Linda@TheRespectedWoman

"Begin somewhere;
you cannot build a reputation
on what you intend to do."
-- Liz Smith

How this book came to be written:

I was having coffee with Valerie Rawls one day, and we were discussing my next book, *The Respected Woman*.

When Valerie walks into a room, heads turn, and you just *know* that she will not put up a lot of nonsense from anyone. I'm said to have a similar effect. "Why?" we asked each other, "do some of us get respect automatically without even thinking about it, and some women never get it?"

There were no answers that day, but the more I thought about it, the more I wanted to know. I started out contacting famous women to ask them how they got where they are. And that led me to broadening my scope because, I reasoned, there were a lot of stories out there -- not just *famous women stories* but stories from all kinds of women -- and I wanted to hear the spectrum.

I was on a very tight deadline in order to have this book available at a marketing conference, so I did most initial contacts by e-mail. Some people who are not fans of e-mail or who were out-of-town didn't even know about this project until it was done. The interviews, over 60 of them, were done in four days. My head swam, but my goodness the things I learned!

> Glory is fleeting,
> but obscurity is forever.
> --Napoleon Bonaparte

I learned a lot that was counterintuitive:

It surprised me how many successful women have been married a long time, and how many had children, and how much those women focused on those children and cherished their marriages.

You'll find many of these women have advanced degrees; some of them have several. I was surprised at how many women have achieved great success primarily through self-education and guts.

One would have expected high achieving women to all be "first children." Some are, and some are middle children and some are the youngest in the family. The usual rules don't seem to apply here.

You always hear tales about competition and scrambling for the top. These women talk about cooperation, sharing, and helping other women. They are creating a new model for success.

They say that volunteerism is dead. Most of these women have a strong record of "giving back".

Conventional wisdom would tell you that high achieving women are all Daddy's girls. Some were, but just as many had no father figure it all.

So many women told me that they were just ordinary women with a dream and the willingness to do whatever it took to make a dream a reality. And they kept on keeping on until they got there.

Over and over again, inevitably just when I thought I had reached my own personal limits, someone would say some variation of, "I just kept going until it was done."

> "I hit the wall and found a way to go under it, over it or around it."

> "I endured discomforts."

> "A professional does what needs to be done, when it needs to be done, whether or not she feels like."

Even a slow learner has to get that message!

If there is one single thing these women have in common it is self-respect.

Our greatest glory is not in never failing,
but in rising up every time we fail.
Ralph Waldo Emerson

The stories I heard!

Our interviews were supposed to last about 10 minutes; few were done in less than 30 minutes; many lasted longer. On one day I did 22 interviews and, while I ended up limp, I was entranced with the modesty, self-deprecating humor, and a sense of connection these women generated.

They told me about their journeys into self-growth and the unknown. Many were forced to achieve by circumstances beyond their control. Many could have settled for mediocrity, and chose not to. They all stretched beyond experience, beyond comfort, and beyond what they thought they were capable of. The message I personally received is, "Stay on the path and you'll eventually get there."

Theresa Bennett-Wilkes told me about being the first baby born on New Year's Day, but all the prizes, all the presents and all the press went to the baby born 10 minutes later-- who was white.

SaraRuth Barger told me about all-girls school near Cleveland that was created for girls that we would currently call "at risk." They had strict rules: academically, socially and morally. These girls left school not only well educated but well prepared for marriage, entertaining, and a career. And this was in the mid-40s!

Stephanie Volo and Nicole Williams each told me about creating a sense of team. They are of a similar age, on opposite sides of the country, and they both possess a drive to achieve that leaves you breathless. I know the next generation of business in America is in good hands.

There were stories about leadership being discovered in little girls of 6, 8, or 10 years old. I heard about character defining moments in children as young as three, which painted a clear picture of whom they would become.

I clearly remember being not quite five years old and getting my first two-wheeled bicycle with training wheels. I got on that bike and I knew how to ride it almost immediately. No problem. No wobbles. And I said to my Daddy, "Take the training wheels *off*, Daddy. I can ride a bicycle all by myself." He said, "Yes, Baby."

I woke up the next morning to find the training wheels were still on the bicycle. When Daddy came home from work, I said again, "Please take the training wheels off the bicycle, Daddy. *I can ride it all by myself.*" He replied again, "Yes, Baby."

I woke up the following morning and again, the training wheels were still in place. I found a hammer and wrench in my father's toolbox, and I proceeded to remove the training wheels. I'll admit it was not a very neat job, but the training wheels *were* removed.

When my father arrived home and saw the bicycle, sans training wheels and some paint, he was livid. "*Linda Jean*! I told you I'd take them off! Why didn't you wait? " I put my little hands on my four-year-old hips, looked him right in the eye and replied, "I asked you *twice*." Yes, indeed, it is very obvious who we'll become even before we go to school.

Cokie Roberts told me about taking needlework to meetings-- it just blew men's minds! Men seldom understood how she could do something with her hands and pay attention to the meeting at the same time. She said, "Like most women, I can

multi-task!" She also said that men go to meetings to *meet* and women go to meetings to *get things done.* She said, "They (men) would just be going on and on and on and I would think to myself, 'I could be folding socks.'" *Do I hear an "AMEN"?* She also said the needlework came in handy at some confrontational meetings where she could stab the canvas rather the speaker. Sublimation is a good thing.

Rita Canning told me about going to meetings with potential sponsors for a domestic violence shelter that she was determined to build. She said, "I was so determined to build it that I was willing to put up my own money if need be. And I walked into every meeting with three backup plans in mind if they said no to me." "Three backup plans?" "Yes," she said. "When I am determined, I will find a way."

All of those stories and more wait for another book.

This will probably surprise you -- I know it surprised me-- there was very little discussion of men. And what there was, for the most part, was positive. I intentionally kept my questions neutral so is not to color the responses. I asked everyone the same six questions:

1. Do you generally feel respected as a woman?

2. What is your own personal definition of "respect?"

3. Is respect something you had to consciously work to achieve?

4. What did you do differently than most women to get where you are?

5. Are the factors that create respect at work the same as those that create respect at home?

6. What would advise women to do to be taken seriously -- by men and by women?

The chicken or the egg?

For women who succeed and achieve, having a good man in her life is a lovely and wonderful by-product of high self-esteem. *Their men listen to them.* Their men are often truly partners who not only provide emotional nourishment but also hold up their end of running the house! Many have been married for over 20 years.

One has to wonder-- did they just get lucky and find a rare man? Or was there something about the woman herself, her standards, her expectations and her willingness to stand up for herself that defines the kind of relationship she has with men. My mother used to say, "There are certain things up with which I will not put."

I assumed there would be a bit of a man-bashing, but not so. It quickly became apparent that high achieving women felt that the opinions of men were just that: *opinions.* As a child, when I would go home to mother, complaining about some-one calling me names, she would say, "And if I called you a teapot, Honey, would you *be* a teapot?" The opinions of other people only have power if you choose to believe them. *And it is a choice.*

It goes without saying
that you should never have more children
than you have car windows.
--Erma Bombeck

I found consensus on several items:

1. All respect for others starts with respect for self – and "like" is something else entirely.

2. Respect is a natural by-product of achievement. And the achievement can be anything you do well, from raising children to being Chief of Staff for a U.S. Congressman.

3. You get taken seriously by others -- including men -- when you take yourself seriously, dress and act like the person you want to become.

4. Be at least as polite and considerate to those you love as you are to strangers.

5. You must have personal boundaries, you must give up playing victim, and you must abandon "baggage."

6. Men respect women who are less emotional and more business-like.

7. Women need to support other women.

8. Taking time for yourself, to exercise, meditate, pray, think, eat and bathe is NOT selfish; merely sensible. After all, what happens to *them* if *you* fall apart?

"A dream is just a dream.
A goal is a dream with a plan and a deadline."
Harvey Mackay

Now it's time for you hear
the real stories from real women.

Many are just like you;
many have lived lives
that are far removed from yours.

I've laughed with these women
and cried with them and *for* them.
You will too.

This is what they had to say . . .

Michele Acquart

Do you generally feel respected as a woman?
Yes, I really do. I've never felt oppression or any barrier to doing whatever I wanted to do.

What is your own personal definition of "respect"?
Respect is a privilege earned as a reflection of how you see your self.

What did you do differently than most women to get where you are?
I never stopped, I never took "no," I never gave up. Never stop trying to do your best. The Universe always has a way for us. I don't know that I'm so different from most women. The women I am close to have similar drive and accountability. Accountability is the biggest difference I see between happy/successful women and those who are not. When one learns (really learns) to take responsibility for EVERY action and event in our lives, then we live powerfully. We are not victims, but co-creators of our destiny.

Was respect something you had to consciously work to achieve?
No. I really learned my lessons from Mom. You can ask for respect but it's really a result of your actions, how you carry yourself, what you put out and a function of hard work. If there is an issue, deal with it now and be direct.

Are the factors that create respect at work the same as those that create respect at home?
Basically yes. In both places you need to speak clearly, expect good results and stay the course. It must be earned in both

environments and is a direct result of the energy we put out and expect in return.

What would you advise women to do to be taken seriously – by men and women?
♀ Always be interesting and always be a resource.
♀ Know your stuff and do your best.

Words of Wisdom

That which does not kill me will serve to make me stronger.
(Laughing!)"Wouldn't take nothin' for my journey now." says Maya Angelou, and learn from your experiences.

Michelle Sanders Acquart: BA Texas Tech University (double major in Spanish and Radio/Television), ½MBA from University of Texas, San Antonio. Fluent in Spanish.

Currently a Senior (experienced-not old!) Account Executive with Hispanic Broadcasting Corporation. This position involves developing results-oriented promotions for clients, managing transactional advertising accounts, creating commercial campaigns all targeted to the majority Hispanic Market in San Antonio, Texas. I job-share this position with my business partner. Each of us works in the office three days a week, with both of us there on Wednesdays. We have to be very organized and detailed to make this work and it does. We are the leading or second leading billers in our market. It affords us a real personal/family life outside of our careers and keeps us fresh and ready to come to work!

I also invest in and manage our rental properties and maintain and manage my costume jewelry business, which does

trade shows. I started my costume jewelry business in 1987 and at one time had six stores and a nationwide mail-order catalog. When the industry declined, I downsized and kept the business active with direct marketing at trade shows and wholesale sales.

Family situation - FABULOUS! Married to Michael Acquart, soul mate and partner. After knowing each other for 16 years we married at 39! After three miscarriages we discovered our path to creating our family was adoption. We first adopted our son, Alexander (Sasha) from Russia (Siberia) in January of 1998 at the age of 13 months. We came back from Russia pregnant again, quickly miscarried and decided to go find our little girl in China. In August of 1999 we brought home our daughter, Annie from Jiang Xi, China at the age of 9 months. They are exquisitely beautiful children and we were certainly all meant to be together. They are very powerful beings. We share our home with Shakespeare and Romeo the dogs and Pearl and Lancelot, the cats. We are usually fostering an animal we find!

Born December 18, 1955. All Sagittarius! Born in Dallas, Texas. Adopted and taken home the day after birth (pre-arranged private adoption) to Dr. O.P. and Mrs. Mary Anne Smith Sanders. Dad died at age 42 when I was only 15 months old. Mom and I were incredibly close. She died at the age of 69 and I miss her still. I am an only child with lots of cousins (with whom I am still retain close ties). I did subsequently find my birth mother and met my two half birth-brothers. This was an interesting adventure I brought into my life, but ultimately I feel no strong personal tie or emotional bond to my birth family, only to my real family.

Debbie Allen

Do you generally feel respected as a woman?
Yes, but it has taken time to earn that respect.

What is your own personal definition of "respect"?
You know you're respected when people look at you as an expert.

What did you do differently than most women to get where you are?
I have never applied for a job, I have no collegeand I started in the family business. At 19, I asked to buy into the family business because I wanted to prove myself. Eventually I got respect from my Dad and changed his perspective on women, but I was in my 40s before that happened. And I have been lucky enough to have good mentors along the way. My dad even asks me for business advice today!

Was respect something you had to consciously work to achieve?
Yes. I was told I was crazy to think I could run a business. I'm a serial entrepreneur! (Laughing) I love to start new business ventures, but I have also learned that you must have a strong focus to take it from idea to success. I believe the power of focus is a wonderful strength that many women have over men. It makes sense since we can easily multi-task and get many things accomplished successfully.

As a speaker, I have to earn respect every time I turn on my microphone. I'm "cute" and people are always surprised that I know my stuff. As an international professional speaker, not only do I present to thousands of men each year, I also pre-

sent in many countries to different cultures as well. Some countries are harder than others to earn respect from men. Since I am a short, attractive blonde I have to overcome stereotypes every time I walk up to the platform to speak. Once they discover that I am very well informed, the expert on the topic, fun and down to earth too, I gain the attention and respect from every man in the room quickly. I think a man will also respect a woman that is not only smart, but warm and approachable as well.

Are the factors that create respect at work the same factors as those that create respect at home?
I live alone and I have no problem with my cat.... she's a girl (Laughing). As a successful and confident woman I often intimidate men. Therefore, that does affect my personal life and long-term relationships. It is not easy to find a great guy that honestly wants a strong successful independent woman. But if you find one send him my way ... *please*! (Laughing!)

What would you advise women to do to be taken seriously – by men and women?
- ♀ Create a strong belief system.
- ♀ First respect yourself -- then others. Believe in yourself and don't take yourself too seriously.
- ♀ Hang out with positive people and rid yourself of anyone that puts you down or drains your energy. Life is too short to surround yourself with negative people. Respect yourself ... your body, beauty and brains.
- ♀ Build strong business alliances and seek out and act on opportunities to promote yourself on a daily basis.
- ♀ Communicate better and carefully choose what you do.
- ♀ Become a shameless self-promoter. Promote your expertise to everyone you meet. Not to serve yourself - but to serve others. When you do what you love and it helps other people you should tell more people about it so you

can help them too. That is successful self-promotion. Help others, support others and send other people that you respect lots of business. The universe will reward you and bring it back your way many times over.

Ask 50 percent more than you're asking now. Ask for what you want - don't wait for others to offer When you negotiate, go for win-win. Get in the habit of ASKING for more in your personal and professional life. When you ASK 50% more than you are right now you are guaranteed so much more out of life, be happier and more successful.

Debbie Allen, Author of *Confessions of Shameless Self-Promoters* **www.DebbieAllen.com**

Debbie Allen has built and sold seven companies although she has never attended a day of college or ever applied for a job in her life. She has achieved success many times over and now inspires others to do the same. Today, as an international professional speaker, she has presents to thousands of people from around the world in numerous countries.

Debbie is the author of three books on business marketing including her bestseller, *Confessions of Shameless Self Promoters* ™ now published in four languages and her latest book, *Confessions of Shameless Internet Promoters.*

Debbie is the recipient of the National Chamber of Commerce Blue Chip Enterprise Award for overcoming business obstacles and achieving fast business growth. She is also the founder of Self-Promotion Month (October) and Business Image

Improvement Month (May) and has been featured in *Who's Who of Marketing Experts* for 2002 & 2003.

Debbie is past president of **National Speaker Association,** Arizona and is a frequent guest on dozens of syndicated radio & TV talk shows throughout the U.S. and Canada. She is the editor of two online newsletters and has been published in dozens of national and international publications including *Entrepreneur, Franchising, Selling Power* and *Sales & Marketing Excellence.*

I'm single and have a cat named Princess Katarina. I was born May 7 and grew up in Indiana just outside of Chicago - lived there until my early 30's then moved to Arizona for a lifestyle change and warm weather. I am the youngest. My older brother owns highly successful businesses back in Indiana.

Good people do not need laws
to tell them to act responsibly,
while bad people
will find a way around the laws.
--Plato

Kristin J. Arnold

Do you generally feel respected as a woman?
Yes.

What is your own personal definition of "respect"?
I think of respect on a couple of levels. Internally: You possess an intrinsic understanding of who you are. If you respect yourself, then you can respect others. Externally: Do others respect you? You are respected when you do what you say you will do, follow through on promises, and act as a "servant leader" for the benefit of others. You go above and beyond what is needed or expected. You understand what it feels like to be in others' shoes. You try to make a difference in others' lives. Don't go looking for respect...you'll find others will respect you when you respect yourself first and respect and believe in others.

What did you do differently than most women to get where you are?
1) I have made a habit of doing things differently. For example, I graduated from the United States Coast Guard Academy. Not a whole lot of Californians went to the Coast Guard Academy, much less a woman! That was very different when I did it.

2) When I am presented with a challenge, I ask, "How am I going to deal with this?" Not **if**, only when and how. And then I just go do it.

3) I am a pathological planner. I strongly believe that planning prevents problems from happening later on. I planned my first business on a cocktail napkin, and it grew from there! Successful people plan for the good

and the bad things that happen, and are better prepared to handle the bumps on the road.

4) I was also willing to seek out and get the support and perspective of others. I strongly believe in the power of teamwork, and I rely heavily on the advice and counsel of my mentors, friends and advocates.

Was respect something you had to consciously work to achieve?
No, not on a conscious level - perhaps unconsciously. For example, I was one of the first women at the Coast Guard Academy as well as on my first ship. I just focused on doing the best job I could and to be the best person I could be. People respect congruency between your talk and your walk - between what you say and what you do. It all has to match.

Are the factors that create respect at work the same factors as those that create respect at home?
Yes, I think the factors are the same; however, we tend to be less guarded at home, less focused on those factors that contribute to respect. Ironically, we can be less respected and respectful with the ones we love the most! Because we want a safe, comfortable place to let our hair down, we don't pay as much attention to all the little details and nuances that make up this word called "respect."

What would you advise women to do to be taken seriously – by men and women?
♀ Don't work too hard at getting taken seriously.
♀ Do the best job you can.
♀ Don't be paranoid - "they" are not out to get you. Most people are too worried about themselves to worry about you too!
♀ Recognize that the world does not revolve around you.
♀ Look for the good and the positive in every situation.

Thoughtfully define what success means to you personally: Is success money, spiritual wholeness, or family relation-

WOW!
Words of Wisdom

ships? Create this definition holistically and do not depend upon the definition of others. After you define success, establish points of reference and check in regularly. Have something that will give you feedback. It might be a visual representation, it might be a mentor, or it might be a mastermind group.

Kristin Arnold: Married since 1983 to Richard L. Arnold, the love of my life. Our son Travis was born 1988 just one pound, two ounces. A modern miracle. Daughter Marina was born in 1991 and is cursed with both my husband's and my desire to excel. Dog, Shadow, a great American black dog

I was born December fifth and raised in a suburb of Los Angeles, Encino, CA. One sister and two brothers - I'm the youngest.

Kristin J. Arnold, CMC, CPF, CSP **www.qpcteam.com** helps corporations, government and non-profit organizations achieve extraordinary results. With years of team-building and facilitation experience, Kristin specializes in coaching executives and their leadership, management and employee teams, particularly in the areas of strategic, business and project planning, process improvement, decision-making, and collaborative problem solving.

In addition to facilitation services, QPC Inc. offers diversified programs around the team concept to meet the needs of CEOs, COOs, executives, managers and team members. Her highly customized speeches and seminars have become in-

strumental in achieving higher performance and results within the workplace.

As a master facilitator, Kristin also trains other facilitators. *"I train your people to do what I do – facilitate teams to higher levels of performance*

An accomplished author and editor of several professional articles and books, as well as a featured columnist in *The Daily Press*, a Tribune Publishing newspaper, Kristin is regarded as an expert in team development and process improvement techniques. Her experience and renowned passion for extraordinary teams have enabled her to build a solid clientele, primarily through referrals, that extends throughout North America and Europe.

Kristin graduated with high honors from the United States Coast Guard Academy. She also earned a Master of Business Administration degree, with an emphasis on Marketing Strategy, from St. Mary's College in California, again graduating with high honors.

♀ American Society of Training and Development, National
& local
♀ Downtown Hampton Development Partnership,
    Past President
♀ Institute of Management Consultants, National
♀ International Association of Facilitators, National
♀ National Speakers Association, National; State Chapter
    Past President

SaraRuth Barger

Do you generally feel respected as a woman?
Yes, I do. People look at me and see my sense of accomplishment. I'm always smiling and I'm not afraid of people. They tend to think I'm knowledgeable.

What is your definition of "respect"?
I think of respect as admiration for someone. Some people I don't like but I admire what they do. Bearing, how you hold yourself, also comes into play.

What did you do differently than most women to get where you are?
I'm very big on balance in your life. I learned self-worth, chutzpah, vulnerability and I gently fought back against being held back. I didn't cave in ; I didn't go with the masses. For a long time I was a follower when I knew I could be a leader.

In my own company, Barger's Weight Management, and Barger Consulting, (Teaching Leaders to Communicate) the most important thing I did differently, was to realize that I made the decisions to be a support person, not a subserviant person. These are two different things.

Now as the District Governor of Toastmasters in North Carolina, I am again running a small business. There are over 2,500 Toastmasters, 120 clubs in NC, and I am in reality their CEO, running this not-for-profit international organization, by the leadership skills I used in my businesses. Again, you lead by example, not by pulling, not by pushing, but by walking beside and doing it together.

Was respect something you had to consciously work to achieve?

I think I did. I learned to respect myself and to believe in my dream and myself.

Are the factors that create respect at work the same as those that create respect at home?
Yes, with the exception that the people at home are supposed to love you. (Laughing) You have to help others solve their own hurts with nurturing. You ask, "How can I help you find your answer?" The concept is the same at work and at home -- the specifics might be different. They must respect you so that you can help them.

What would you advise women to do to be taken seriously – by men and women?
- ♀ Develop good posture, physical graces and self-confidence. Know what you need to know and ask when you need to.
- ♀ Follow through and never lie. You lead by example--being sure the decision you make is good for all.
- ♀ Be **Wise**
- ♀ Be **Open**
- ♀ Be **Wonderful** --- that's a...

WOW!
Words of Wisdom

SaraRuth Barger: Education: Andrews School for Women in Willoughby, Ohio--a school far ahead of its time. Founded to provide young girls and women with an education, a career base and the social graces required to survive at home and in the world. At the time, only girls from broken homes or mother-less homes were admitted. My Mother died when I was four. It was a boarding school from 7th -12th grades. I credit Andrews for making me the woman I have become.

I've worked in retailing, factories, doctors' offices, banking, as a stay at home Mom, Ideal Diet Company, Barger's Weight Management, and Barger Consulting.

I married a ministerial student and the first seven years as a pastor's wife was a culture shock to me. I was raised at Andrews to be the important one, to choose my own profession, not follow my husband's choice. But as a Pastor's wife, there were lines I could not cross in the denominations we followed in Indiana and Michigan.

Born: July 6, 1931 in Cleveland Ohio-grew up in Ohio and Indiana with two older brothers, Charles and William – and I'm **still growing up** in North Carolina. Married to Harold E. Barger. Children: John V. Barger, Leah M. Barger, Scott V. Barger, Mark A. Barger. seven Grandchildren: five by blood and two by heart, 1 great-granddaughter. Pets: Dogs when children were home. Cats for me! Mittins, for 13 years and ABU for one year.

We either make ourselves miserable
or we make ourselves strong.
The amount of work is the same.
- Carlos Castaneda

Dena Higgins Barnes

Do you generally feel respected as a woman?
Yes, I do. There are certain times when we all feel we're not respected as people. This is still a man's world in politics, but yes, I feel respected for the most part.

What is your definition of "respect"?
People listen to you and value what you say and do. If others ask questions, it gives you a chance to clarify something they may not agree with. People listen to you and try to understand where you're coming from.

What did you do differently than most women to get where you are?
I persevered, I kept going, I ignored the nay-sayers who said, "It can't be done." I don't believe that things can't be done, I believe that things are not always successful, and as we try to do things we certainly grow, broaden our horizons, and learn understanding. I think when there's something that really seems important we must just persevere and strive to get the things that we feel are important DONE.

Was respect something you had to consciously work to achieve?
After being on the Summerfield town council for six years, I was elected mayor of the council. I did have to consciously work toward getting respect. Early on they treated me like I was a dummy, and there is a tremendous learning curve. You have to understand that when you're elected to public office, everything takes more time and more effort than you believe it will. When a woman's in politics, people often treat you -- and that's usually men -- like you're a little girl.

Are the factors that create respect at work the same as those that create respect at home?

That's interesting to ponder. The factors that engender respect are the same universally: people are entitled to their own beliefs. The situations may be different. Your respect at work often has to do with your knowledge, your professional manner. At home it's more about how you treat others and what you say. It all has to do with how you deal with people; how you treat them and lots of times you resent it when people don't meet your expectations. We all have our expectations of people that they will treat us fairly and honestly in a manner that is accepting. They seem to be the same factors.

What would you advise women to do to be taken seriously – by men and women?

Stop and *think* about what you're going to say. Enthusiasm and spontaneity are very good but before you speak, plan your statement so that you will not accidentally offend or be misconstrued.

WOW!
Words of Wisdom

What you have deep within you is the love that God has given all of us. Let it shine through. Don't be distracted by the little things. Remember what you really want to accomplish and keep your eye on the goal.

Dena Higgins Barnes: Mayor of Summerfield, North Carolina, third largest town in Guilford County.
Served on Summerfield Town Council since 1997

Married to BJ Barnes, Guilford County Sheriff since 1994, two daughters and five grandchildren. My mother, 87, lives with us and BJ's parents live behind us. We have an 11-year-old Doberman "Diamond" who still acts like a puppy

Born in Greensboro, North Carolina and grew up in Summerfield with one older sister. Graduated from Grimsley High School in 1969 and Guilford Technical Community College in 1979 with an associate degree in Nursing. Worked in Med/Surg nursing and cardiac unit at Moses Cone Hospital for 8 years. Worked in a physician's office for 12 years.

You gain strength, courage and confidence
by every experience in which you really stop
to look fear in the face.
You are able to say to yourself,
"I lived through this horror.
I can take the next thing that comes along." . . .
You must do the thing you think you cannot do.
- Eleanor Roosevelt

Theresa W. Bennett-Wilkes

Do you generally feel respected as a woman?
Yes, I do - and I don't - depending upon the situation. As a child of God, yes. Sometimes ... in other situations, no.

What is your own personal definition of respect?
An appreciation of a person who has a good value system; one that I can embrace. Someone who lives his or her life with integrity, has a good heart, no pretensions, says what she or he means and means what she or he says.

What did you do differently than most women to get where you are?
I made a deliberate decision to *do it.* I had a very altruistic view of writing as a career. It was something in the back of my mind that I didn't see as viable. I had encouragement to become a writer, but I wasn't interested initially. When I discovered that what I *thought* I really wanted to do was no longer an option, I began writing as a means of escape. It was my way of dealing with depression and frustration. I discovered that I loved writing and had a real passion for it. Becoming a writer was a decision I had to make, and choosing it as my career was my choice. I didn't get here by accident.

Was respect something you had to consciously work to achieve?
Yes. I am a well-educated, articulate African-American woman. I live in a society that hasn't always recognized my right to be what I am. I believe we're all entitled to success, respect, cooperation and appreciation. When you encounter disrespect, I think it's important to understand where it's

coming from so that you can deal with it in a manner that *dignifies you.*

Are the factors that create respect at work the same factors as those that create respect at home?
No, at work they don't know me as well as my family does. Respect at work has more variables: your position, your education, and your expectations.

What would you advise women to do to be taken seriously – by men and women?
♀ Some people will automatically respond well to you, based on how you present yourself. Learn to deal positively and assertively with people who don't take you seriously.
♀ Choose your battles. You can't have your integrity and righteous indignation, too.
♀ Don't identify yourself in terms of your husband, lover, significant other, children, or your work. Be proud of who you are - you've earned those years.
♀ Please stop using the term, "my boyfriend" after you're 25.
♀ We raise plants and animals, not children. We rear our children.
♀ Whatever you do in this life has to be worth getting out of bed for!
♀ Support other women and women's causes. We shouldn't still be battling for the right to choose anything!!!

Do things that grown-up women do: Get a mortgage, earn a living doing what you like, not what you feel you have to do; buy a car, travel to foreign countries, volunteer in your community, develop hobbies and learn to value your

friends. It makes a huge difference in your choices when you take complete ownership of your own life!

Theresa Bennett-Wilkes: I am a freelance commercial and literary writer, in private practice. I am also a published author. *A Taste of Theresa: Musings From My Point of View* is available through Holly Tree Publications, LLP (336) 841-7841 or **www.alwaystheresa.com**. I've written for the *Carolina Peacemaker* and the *Winston-Salem Journal*, and have a growing body of work. I'm a former basic skills instructor with Guilford Technical Community College.

B.A. in Social Studies from Bennett College, Greensboro, 1972, Master of Urban Planning Degree, University of Washington, Seattle, 1978. Twenty + years as an urban planner, including three years as a Senior Planning Officer, Ipswich Borough Council, Ipswich, Suffolk, England. I am a retired member of the Royal Town Planning Institute, United Kingdom of Great Britain, Scotland, Northern Ireland and Wales.

I am married to Msgt Willie Lee Wilkes, United States Air Force, Retired. We have one daughter, Kamilah. I was born January 1, 1950 and am very proud of that. I have earned these years, and I claim them…most days, anyway.

I was born in Yakima, WA to the late Rev. Everett P. Williams, Sr. and Mrs. Blanche G. Williams. I grew up in Oakland, CA and I am a product of the California Public Schools. I have two younger brothers. Everett, Jr., a graduate of Oberlin Conservatory of Music, is Minister of Music at Hartford Memorial Baptist Church, Detroit, MI. Allen, my youngest brother is Rev. Dr. Allen L. Williams, Pastor of Bethel African Methodist Episcopal Church, Kansas City, MO. I have two wonderful sisters-in-law, Marcheta Williams and Glenda Rawls and quite a few nieces and nephews.

Lenora Billings-Harris, CSP

Do you generally feel respected as a woman?
I generally do feel respected. When I am among mostly women, I feel included and respected. Among men in my professional field I feel equal. When I wear my Mrs. Harris hat, I sometimes feel discounted.

What is your own personal definition of "respect"?
The ability to say what needs to be said in a way that others can hear it and retain a positive relationship. (That's my life mission!) It is also respectful to get to know the essence of the other person. When I speak my truth, I get respect.

What did you do differently than most women to get where you are?
I learned early to carry myself in such a way that others wouldn't take advantage of me. As a result, I've heard others say that my personality style which is a positive, enthusiastic, very confident *façade* (Laughing!) initially seems off-putting until they get to know me.

Was respect something you had to consciously work to achieve?
I don't think so. I was a leader even as a child. Throughout my life others have seen qualities in me before I saw them in myself. I've often attracted sponsors who have believed in me and made my path easier.

Are the factors that create respect at work the same factors as those that create respect at home?
Basically yes. Your own level of self-esteem and respect at home are the same as at work. You need to be authentically

you regardless of the environment. The more I allow myself to just be me, the more respect I get.

What would you advise women to do to be taken seriously – by men and women?
It is a given that you have to be very good at what you do if you want to get ahead.

Get over being "cute." Make a clear decision, based on established rules, about how you want to present yourself, about how you want to look at work, how you want to sound and how you want to interact with other people. Erin Brockovich may have found fame and glory with short skirts and cleavage but unnless you're in a position to make the rules, you may not.

Listen to your "heart voice," and follow its advice.

Lenora Billings-Harris, CSP: Whether through keynotes, half-day workshops, or multi-day seminars, Lenora's thought-provoking presentations are lively, positive, and non-judgmental. Using marbles and other fun metaphors, she will help your group discover how to: Create a respectful workplace that values differences , S.T.O.P. inappropriate behavior and preserve the relationship, Counteract stereotypical beliefs affecting productivity

Lenora Billings-Harris is an international speaker, and author of <u>The Diversity Advantage: A Guide to Making Diversity Work</u>. (**www.lenoraspeaks.com**) Since 1986, she has helped people solve diversity dilemmas, and organizations improve

productivity in a multicultural environment. Her clients include Fortune 500 companies as well as educational institutions and professional associations. She serves on the Board of the *National Speakers Association*, and is an adjunct professor at the University of North Carolina-Greensboro.

Lenora's Most Popular Topics Include:

The Power IS You! A Wizard of Oz Perspective

This unique keynote uses the Wizard of Oz characters as a metaphor to help you use your brain, heart and courage to make a real difference in today's multicultural world. This thought-provoking message inspires audiences to increase their options for success, by embracing the gifts they each possess.

The Diversity Advantage: Turning Barriers into Bridges

You will learn how, when and why people rely on stereotypes to make day-to-day decisions about others. You will leave with specific ideas for action to improve your multicultural relations.

Empowering Teams by Valuing Differences

Learn the four critical elements necessary for team effectiveness while you unlock your preconceived notions about others. This highly interactive session will equip you with tools and techniques for immediate application.

From Adversaries to Allies: Gender Communication in the Workplace

This fun presentation will help both men and women learn how to improve their communication with the opposite gender. Say what you mean and get what you want while recognizing differences.

Birthday- August 9, 1950. I am proud of my age. I don't hide it. Married: 28 years this summer.

Paula Jorde Bloom

Do you generally feel respected as a woman?
Yes absolutely.

What is your own personal definition of "respect"?
Mutual regard.

What did you do differently than most women to get where you are?
I believe I work hard to empower others. Their success has surely contributed to my own success. I think most people would say I have a strong sense of self and an internal locus of control. I take responsibility for my own actions and set high expectations for myself. While I value input and feedback from those around me, I do not let external influences define my self worth. In other words, I have set my own indicators for measuring success, happiness, and fulfillment. I'm also not afraid to take charge of change. I have an uncompromising passion about my work and a high energy level.

Was respect something you had to consciously work to achieve?
No, not consciously. However, I've always been very conscious of my behavior and its impact on others. I believe being liked and being respected are two different things. I have a desire to be liked, but I would rather be respected. People like you when you meet their needs. People respect you when you are trustworthy, follow through on commitments, and behave with integrity.

Are the factors that create respect at work the same factors as those that create respect at home?
They're different but certainly have some overlapping characteristics. At home I think it is important to have a playful spirit, be patient, flexible, available, and sensitive to the shifting moods and needs of others. Being a good listener and being consistent in actions and expectations is also crucial. Finally, I think on the home front it's essential that you be an enthusiastic cheerleader for everyone's small and big accomplishments.

While relationships at home and at work are both based on trust, I think the nature of the trust factor is different. At home, I believe trust is assumed and expected. It is automatically there by virtue of our relationship with our spouse and children. We can sustain that trust or destroy that trust, but we start out from a base and expectation that trust is there. At work, I think trust needs to be earned. It doesn't automatically come with the job title or role.

Respect is a natural outgrowth of a trusting relationship. In the workplace, respect comes when you walk the talk, presume positive intentions, operate from a base of mutual regard, show compassion, and demonstrate integrity in words and deeds. Respect is further enhanced when you exhibit good judgment, seek consensus, and display an optimistic spirit. In the end, I believe the people who garner the most respect, though, are those who have a higher calling in life than merely satisfying personal wants and needs.

What would you advise women to do to be taken seriously – by men and women?
I'm not sure I like this question because it implies women should be focused on external judgments for defining their self worth. The best way to be taken seriously is not to worry about being taken seriously. You'll never please everyone.

WOW!
Words of Wisdom

Find your own North Star and let that be your guide. That's where true authenticity comes from. If you know what you stand for and genuinely seek to understand others' perspectives and differing points of view, respect will usually follow.

Paula Jorde Bloom is a Professor of Early Childhood Education and Director of the Center for Early Childhood Leadership at National-Louis University in Wheeling, Illinois.

As one of the country's leading experts on early childhood leadership and program management issues, Dr. Bloom is a frequent keynote speaker at state, national, and international conferences and consultant to professional organizations and state agencies.

Paula received her master's and doctoral degrees from Stanford University. She has taught preschool and kindergarten, designed and directed a childcare center, and served as administrator of a campus laboratory school. Her current research interests are in the areas of organizational climate and occupational stress as they relate to indices of job satisfaction in early childhood settings. Dr. Bloom is the author of numerous journal articles and several widely read books including *Avoiding Burnout, A Great Place to Work, Blueprint for Action, Circle of Influence, Making the Most of Meetings,* **and** *Workshop Essentials.*

Family situation
I am married to Darrell Bloom. We have four children (three from Darrell's first marriage and one from our marriage). Our oldest daughter, Laura (33) is married and has two

preschool-aged children. Our son, Todd (31) is engaged and will be married next January. Our son Erik (26) lives and works in Minneapolis. Our youngest daughter, Kristine, is in the 6th grade. We have a precious Bischon dog named Chelsea.

Born September 27, 1947 in Detroit, Michigan, moved to southern California (the Mojave Desert) when I was 6. From Detroit to northern California and lived in the San Francisco Bay area until I went to college. I am a middle child sandwiched in between two brothers – the eldest is 17mo older than I; the younger is 5 years younger than I am.

A happy person is not a person
in a certain set of circumstances,
but rather a person
with a certain set of attitudes.
- Hugh Downs

Dr. Judith Briles

Do you generally feel respected as a woman?
Yes. I've got several degrees. (Smile) You have to earn them and respect follows. Women think, "I create my own tools." Men think," Show me."

What is your definition of "respect"?
I feel respected when people are not pre-judgmental, and honor my experience, my person, and my position.

What did you do differently than most women to get where you are?
I was willing to fail, to state my opinions, to stick my neck out, and live with the consequences. As you move up, the more visible you are, the more likely you'll be attacked by those who play power games and/or are envious of your material gains.

Was respect something you had to consciously work to achieve?
It was when I started off as a stockbroker who was fired because I was going through a divorce. (Laughing!) I had 3 kids to feed. I did not consciously go after respect but people respected me for my work and eventually supported me when I started my own business.

Are the factors that create respect at work the same as those that create respect at home?
They overflow. The same mechanisms will work in both arenas.

What would you advise women to do to be taken seriously – by men and women?

♀ Men can respect you without liking you; women seldom can.

♀ Be aware of communication styles and learn how to confront effectively.

♀ Knock off being fluffy, super-sweet Geishas.

♀ Be more overt and direct in your communications and play fewer games.

♀ Respect the differences between men and women.

♀ Learn that everyone is not *friend* material and don't tell all of your secrets to everyone, don't reveal personal information to those who are not personal friends.

♀ Don't gossip

You need to learn how to brag about yourself and pat yourself on the back because people believe what you say about yourself and how you think about yourself.

Dr. Judith Briles: Spouse: John Maling, two adult children Shelley and Sheryl. Born: Feb 20, 1946, in Los Angeles, grew up in Palos Verdes—California. Family of 3 brothers, I'm in the middle.

Dr. Judith Briles is an award winning and best-selling author of 23 books including *The Confidence Factor, Woman to Woman 2000, Zapping Conflict in the Health Care Workplace, 10 Smart Money Moves for Women, GenderTraps* and *The SeXX Factor.* http://www.briles.com

She is featured frequently on radio and television and the Internet sites *MsMoney.com.* Her work and articles have appeared in *The*

Wall Street Journal, USA Today, Time, Money, The New York Times, People and other publications. She has appeared on over 1000 programs including *MSNBC, CNN, CNNfn, Leeza,* and *Oprah.* She writes monthly columns for the *Denver Business Journal* and *Colorado Woman News.*

Dr. Judith Briles is known as a catalyst for change and believes that every pitfall experienced leads to an opportunity and greater success. She is a national director of The WISH List and is a past board member of the **National Speakers Association,** the Women's Bank San Francisco, and the Colorado League of Nursing. Judith is an honorary member of the Association of Women Surgeons and The Women Officers Professional Association. Although she holds both Masters and Doctorate degrees in Business Administration, her *real* degrees come from life.

All the adversity I've had in my life,
all my troubles and obstacles,
have strengthened me...
You may not realize it when it happens,
but a kick in the teeth
may be the best thing in the world for you.
-- Walt Disney

Brett Butler

Do you generally feel respected as a woman?
Sure.

What is your own personal definition of "respect"?
I think it's a quality that is very hard to generate if you don't have it within. It's a self-fulfilling belief about your own ability to be equal in personal and professional situations.

What did you do differently than most women to get where you are?
My success was as inadvertent as it was intentional. In a way, I'm also an inadvertent pioneer. Who knew you could make money off your mouth without a college degree? I was a hard-working accident. It never occurred to me that I was the inferior gender until I was almost 40.

I sort of had blinders on about this dream I had. Early on in life I knew what was most sacred to me. It just pulled me by the seat of the pants into everything. And that's comedy.

Was respect something you had to consciously work to achieve? No, I tried to achieve being funny first, and I knew that there would be a lot of people who would not respect that path, that goal, and many would disagree with what I thought was funny. Who said, "To thine own self be true?" The Oracle of Delphi? My Mother said it was Shakespeare …or Plato …or Ben Franklin…maybe it was Kelly Ripa? (Laughing)

I never sought "respect." I hoped it would be a top-tier by-product of what I did. I always wanted to be as funny as a

man but I didn't want to do uterine comedy. I like what I do. I am a woman. I talk about it. It's in my act, but it *doesn't* come out of.... *"I have tits, hear me roar!"* I never liked that.

Are the factors that create respect at work the same factors as those that create respect at home?
It would break my brain if I thought they were different. I'm not sure if you can have true success in either dimension without paying attention to the other one ...and yet I see it being done in America all the time. We're really stratified.

What advice would you give women to help them get taken seriously?
The answer to that question is so far down the list of what you are doing with your life! If you are cleaving to this beautiful thrum inside yourself about what it is that brings you joy, if you follow your bliss, I promise you... it is more sacred than any path generated or given to you by another human.

If you have this idea that finishing your education is success, or finding the perfect job, or having the perfect house inhabited by the perfect husband and 2.4 children means success...I can almost promise you that unless the things that **get you there** bring you joy.... once you get *there*, you will be miserable. I know that.

If you wait for a goal - whatever it is --to be a nun or to be rich and famous -- to wait for "happy," then you have just screwed yourself out of that key thing.

There is nothing in this short life that feels like being true to yourself. And often, that means that a lot of people won't "get you" and that can't bother you from the get-go, comin' out of the gate.

It's like you're a thoroughbred horse coming out of that gate for the race of your life, and if you're checking out the other horses to see if their silks are prettier than yours...you have just missed the point of being a champion horse.

Be kinder to men, who also carry a burden, take fewer potshots. There is no way I am going to succeed without my brother beside me.

Women, for biological reasons, tend to have a stronger need for peace and we have a vision of it. We need that voice to not be so quiet. We need to pay attention to that voice.

FROM THE AUTHOR:
Brett Butler, probably best known as the star of *Grace Under Fire*, is preparing for the *Gravel Throated Happy Tour*. Since she was seriously over-scheduled and her manager threatened her with extinction if she did this interview, no biographical information is included. So I will just give you my *read* on this lady.

I truly believe that Brett Butler is one of the funniest, deepest, most articulate women I have ever met. She travels from quoting the Oracle of Delphi to dishing about rednecks in one line. She speaks universal truths and down-home homilies with the same reverence and irreverence. Check out www.BrettButler.com to see if she's coming to your town – you won't want to miss her!

Rita Canning

Do you generally feel respected as a woman?
Yes...**not** being respected never occurred to me. (Laughing!)

What is your own personal definition of "respect"?
It's a combination of admiration, and emulation, being asked to be a mentor or a role model.

What did you do differently than most women to get where you are?
I am **very** goal oriented. Nothing deters me. If I run into an obstacle, I will find another way to solve the problem. I will go over it, around it, or under it. When I walk into a difficult situation I have several backup plans ready to go. If you want something bad enough, if you stay focused and you're deter-mined, you'll find a way to get there.

I didn't let emotions get in my way. I am so direct that many times I know I am thought of as tactless. I'm sure I've hurt people's feelings --- but never intentionally. It's just that I of-ten tell the unvarnished truth.

I'm a good risk taker.

Was respect something you had to consciously work to achieve?
I've never thought about it but as a child I equated respect with being "good." And it was important to my parents so it became important to me.

Are the factors that create respect at work the same factors as those that create respect at home?

Yes. Duties, functions, all those things in a job description whether at home or at work, are not respected. The elements of your character get you respect, such as ethics, principals, and morals. If someone cheats on the golf course, he or she will cheat in the boardroom. Are you principled? The answer is yes or no.

What would you advise women to do to be taken seriously – by men and women?

♀ Do your homework and know your stuff. Know who you're speaking to before you open your mouth. Do your homework and find out what your audience will respond to. Some people respect intelligence, others respond to traditional womanly wiles. Present yourself in the way that will bring out the best in the other person.

♀ Be prepared and do not underestimate the other person. Learn how to draw out the other person, ask questions and really listen.

♀ Be self-confident, proud, exuberant and exude energy. It's contagious and attractive!

Words of Wisdom

You have many resources. It might be money; it might be friends, education, experience, personality, abilities, talents, family or connections. Find a way to incorporate your resources into accomplishing your goals.

Rita Canning: I was born in Melrose Park, Illinois, 8/23/42, and grew up in Maywood, Illinois. I had two older brothers. My husband is John A. Canning, Jr., President and Founder of Madison Dearborn Partners in Chicago. I have six children - 3 sons, 2 stepsons and 1 stepdaughter.

Graduated from University of Illinois, Champaign with a B.S. degree from the College of Commerce and Business Administration.

2001 recipient of the Sears Distinguished Leader Award for exemplary volunteer contributions.

Founder of the Palatine Home of the Sparrow, a transitional shelter program for abused and homeless women and their children.

President of the Board of WINGS (Women In Need Growing Stronger) that also provides transitional shelter for abused and homeless women and children.

Currently in the process of establishing the first 24 hour emergency domestic violence shelter in Chicago's northwest suburbs.

Funded and helped to create the Holy Angels Outreach Program to assist disadvantaged inner city families.

Member of the Women's Board of Northwestern University.

Director and Vice-President of The Canning Foundation which funds such programs as The Canning Scholars which provides scholarships to 85 inner-city children to six private schools both elementary and secondary.

There is no try.
There is only do or not do.
Yoda, from The Empire Strikes Back

Linda Chandler

Do you generally feel respected as a woman?
For me, yes, but in the general "men vs. women" arena, I have to say absolutely not. Lack of respect, however, is not always a gender issue.

What is your definition of "respect"?
To be accorded the opportunity to be heard or seen, and given a platform for your ideas to be heard without immediate judgment or disregard.

What did you do differently than most women to get where you are?
I got past my ego. I got beyond being the *little* pretty, *little* bright, *little* accomplished person that people spoke about. And the "little" had nothing to do with my stature. Before I was 10 years old I understood there were no differences based on skin, religion, or ethnicity. I was open to understanding those who are different from me and I had a global perspective.

Was respect something you had to consciously work to achieve?
No.

Are the factors that create respect at work the same as those that create respect at home?
They can be but are not necessarily so and are not mutually exclusive. These two areas of your life are not separate. If you're congruent, you are congruent wherever you are in the fundamental drivers of whatever you are doing.

When your words, your voice, your body and your beliefs all deliver the same message, you are congruent and that commands respect wherever you happen to be.

What would you advise women to do to be taken seriously – by men and women?
Treat others with the respect you want to have accorded to you. Be authentic. Get the results you deserve. Set your high expectations of hope and belief, as you simultaneously remain fully grounded.

My work and relationships have given me the opportunity to travel globally and the dynamics are similar everywhere.

Come from your heart -- and at your heart level be gentle and forgiving to yourself. Be a human who has the capacity to make daily choices that impact others positively.

Linda Chandler: Investment advisor, strategic consultant, entrepreneur, business leader, author, lecturer, and seminar leader. Linda Chandler is an accomplished woman who has achieved extraordinary feats in the world of business and finance at the highest levels. She has been a superstar in three industries--the securities industry and investment banking--and today as a professional speaker and Fortune 500 trainer. See http://www.LindaChandler.com.

Linda is an international authority on capital formation, core value training, sales mastery and fast growth business strategies. Chandler is involved in helping new ventures that are

developing disruptive technology, and gives them a competitive advantage and a well-protected pathway to sustained profitability. Her expertise is advising startups, new ventures, emerging growth companies and turnarounds on strategies to prepare the platform for future growth, profitability, and enhanced value. She also is exceptional at presenting leading-edge programs that focus on values based leadership, personal development training, and MasterMind brain trust collaboration.

As an internationally recognized speaker, Linda Chandler has addressed many national and regional conferences, conventions and meetings across the country and in Europe, Asia, the Pacific region, and Canada. She has shared the platform with notables like Tom Peters, Denis Waitley, Mark Victor Hansen, Jack Canfield, Wayne Huizenga, Bob Proctor, Les Brown, Roger Dawson, Ken Blanchard, Eli Goldratt, Michael Gerber, Dennis Kimbro, Wilson Harrell, Jon Goodman, Scott DeGarmo, and many others

As a Strategic Consultant for numerous early stage companies, she has advised firms in diverse fields from health care to broadcasting, from engineering to retail operations, from service industry to manufacturing, from financial services to network marketing. Working with CEO's, senior management teams, and Boards of Directors, she has architected and successfully implemented full-scale operational and financial turnarounds. Her expertise is repositioning a company as an information-based firm that capitalizes on its human assets, intellectual properties, and information capital. In this process, she weaves in her Core Value Training process that produces transformational results.

Linda was born October 21 in South Dakota and grew up in the Midwest, mainly Iowa, and has two younger brothers.

Sharon Daggers

Do you generally feel respected as a woman?
Yes, but there are always exceptions. (Laughing!)

What is your own personal definition of "respect"?
Within myself respect is about being happy with the choices I make, that allow me to grow to be the best that I can be. I like to feel that I can contribute some part of myself in a positive way. I know, by comparison, of choices I have made in life that I didn't respect.

Respect is also about letting people be who they are. I feel respected when people hear what I say and respect my boundaries. I feel disrespected when I repeatedly have to explain myself. Of course that is not true when one is trying to clarify details for a project. In that case, ask me over and over again until my or your ideas are clear. That shows respect, when people take the time to understand one another.

What did you do differently than most women to get to where you are?
I took the hard way. I was willing to take the risk that I could make a living as an artist in a new area, without the comfortable resources I was accustomed to.

Was respect something you had to consciously work to achieve?
I've learned to respect my choices and myself. Once that is established within oneself, respect comes more naturally from others.

Are the factors that create respect at work the same factors that create respect at home?
Generally yes...those factors are within yourself.

What would you advise women to do to be taken seriously – by men and women?
Take yourself seriously, but keep a sense of humor.

Take an occasional risk!

Sharon Daggers: Born August 6, 1958. I grew up in Bucks County Pennsylvania. I'm one of three children, with a sister two years older and a brother two years younger.

I have two sons, Jeffrey and Jarid. I live alone, but am frequently visited by my son Jarid, who spends his time between Philadelphia and here in High Point N.C. My other son Jeffrey is attending college at Colorado State.

I have pursued art passionately all my life trying to find a way to both live and work creatively. After getting married and having two children I continued taking many different courses to explore the options for a career in art. I focused on all the things I loved and did best., which were art, interior design, and working with people. Doing faux finishes and mural work was the perfect fit in combining those elements.

Moving to High Point, N.C. provided many different possibilities because it is centered on the furniture capital of the world.

I worked for a company creating designs and then painting them on furniture that was shown at the International Furni-

ture Market. This opened the door to painting faux finishes and murals for the showrooms.

Commercial Jobs have included:
Piedmont Environmental Center, Spring Air Mattress, Leon's Hair Salon, Malave Granite and Marble, Piedmont Engineers Of the Carolinas, Distinctive Dwellings, Bliss and Company Salon
Restaurant Murals: M'couls Public House downtown Greensboro, Talk Of The Town Cafe, Greensboro, Lubrano's Italian Restaurant, Greensboro
Furniture Companies: Charlestonforge, Friul Cassetti, Delma Kids, Webb, Bernhardt, Landmark

Education: Bucks County Community College-Newtown, PA. Coursework in fine arts and commercial arts, Philadelphia College of Textiles and Science
Coursework design, computer and color theory

I have a poem printed in *TODAY'S AMERICAN WOMAN*. (Jan.03) and I am currently working on a book of prose with verbal and painted vignettes.

Be willing to be uncomfortable.
Be comfortable being uncomfortable.
It may get tough,
but it's a small price to pay for living a dream.
- Peter McWilliams

Rebecca Snyders Darr

Do you generally feel respected as a woman?
Yes, I do. I felt respected since I was a child.

What is your own personal definition of "respect"?
Listening with your whole mind and body to what others tell you -- no matter their age. Pay attention and honor their input.

What did you do differently than most women to get where you are?
I'm not sure... I was often at the right place at the right time. I kept my eyes open for opportunities, so that I didn't miss any when they came along. I try to always be present mentally and physically.

Was respect something you had to consciously work to achieve?
Not consciously. In new situations I know I always have to prove what I say and earn respect. I've always been surrounded and raised by overachievers and I've had good mentors along the way.

Are the factors that create respect at work the same factors as those that create respect at home?
Yes, without a doubt. Focus on the relationship first and problems second, that way everyone feels respected and problems get solved. Listen carefully and be present during discussions at home and work.

What would you advise women to do to be taken seriously – by men and women?

- ♀ If anyone is capable of doing it, you can too. Remember that no one is better than you are.
- ♀ Let nothing stop you.
- ♀ Keep your eyes open and when you run into a wall, figure at how you can go over it, around it, or under it. Or just go through it. Be unstoppable and look at all problems in new ways.
- ♀ Don't let others hold you down

Motherhood is the most respectable career.

Rebecca Darr: Joe and I have been married 11 years. We started dating as seniors in high school and stayed together through college. We moved to San Jose for 6 years and moved back to Illinois in 1998. In 2000, we had Ben and Luke, identical twins. In 2002, we had Sam. We don't have time for pets!

I was born December 6, 1967 and raised in Alton, Illinois (on the Mississippi River, 20 miles from St. Louis.) I was the second child of four. I have a sister, 14 months older, Betsy, a sister 2 years younger, Bobbi, and a brother 3 ½ years younger, Scott. We were close in age and close in relationship. We still are very close siblings.

Professional Experience
1/99 to Present **The WINGS Program, Inc.** – Arlington Heights, IL (www.WingsProgram.com)

Executive Director, Transitional housing program that provides support and services to homeless women and children to assist them in reaching the goal of permanent housing. The program provides shelter to over fifty women and children each night and requires that all clients gain employment, save 80% of net income for future housing, and fully utilize all services provided.

1992 -98 **Second Start / Pine Hill School** - San Jose, CA
Director of School Programs, Responsible for administration and oversight of all school programs and site functions on two campuses of a non-profit private school for students with severe learning disabilities and behavioral problems.
Director of Youth Services, Counselor

Education: **M.A. Clinical Psychology** - June 1995, John F. Kennedy University - Orinda, CA,
B.S. Psychology - May 1990,University of Illinois at Champaign-Urbana, Graduated with Distinction in Psychology - Honors Program

Task Force on Homelessness in Suburban Cook County- Past Chair, Assoc. of Professional Fundraisers
Illinois Assoc. of Non-Profit Organizations,
Chicago Women in Philanthropy

One must still have chaos
in oneself to give birth to a dancing star.
- Nietzsche

Barbara Davidson

Do you generally feel respected as a woman?
Generally do. I believe it comes with being credible... doing what you like and doing it well. Most of all, I try always to interact with peer/associates in a respectful manner remembering I must first respect myself in order to command respect.

What is your own personal definition of "respect"?
I think of respect in terms of treatment. Is one treated well, out of consideration, equally? Are you treated in the way you want to be treated?

What did you do differently than most women to get where you are?
I'm not sure that I did. Women who have aspirations have to work hard. I was committed to doing it and willing to pay the price.

Was respect something you had to consciously work to achieve?
No, I don't remember doing that. I believe in professionalism and common courtesy. I found that merit and hard work equaled respect.

Are the factors that create respect at work the same as those that create respect at home?
Yes. They are very much the same. It took me a lot of years to "get it"-- that the principles of conduct and treatment of each other have to be consistent throughout your life.

**What would you advise women to do to be taken seriously –
by men and women?**
♀ Dress the part. Present yourself in a professional manner.
♀ Learn to be articulate, to express yourself well, to take a
stand and make hard decisions. Learn how to make sure
that your point is understood and don't be shouted down.

Do what you love to do!

Barbara Davidson: Born in Fort Smith, Arkansas, August 19,
1948. Father a factory worker, mother a housewife. Being the
oldest my Mother entrusted me with a lot of responsibility at
a very early age. I credit her with my strong sense of responsibility or more accurately "take charge attitude."

Divorced many years with two grown children, a son and a
daughter. My daughter is the mother of my two grandchildren. Caleb is age 10 and Madison Grace is 3.

Career of 34 years in Banking or Banking-related fields. Last
14 years I served as a Director, Senior Vice President of Lending Operations for Arvest Bank with assets in excess of 5 bil-
lion. Arvest is a privately held Bank owned by the Walton
family of Wal-Mart. Responsible for the many facets of commercial and consumer lending services provided to 150+
branches in Arkansas, Oklahoma and Missouri. During this
time frame, I was also Chief Operating Officer for Arvest
Mortgage Company.

I have been committed to helping those I have worked with
(most of which are women) to further their careers while bal-
ancing the responsibilities of family. Pursued degrees in So-

ciology and Business Management. Attended AMA Business Management School, New York.

Served on Board for StarPont, Inc., since 1997 – a non-profit organization formed to support women and children to acquire life skills to become productive members of the community.

The secret of getting ahead is getting started.
The secret of getting started
is breaking your complex over-whelming tasks
into small manageable tasks,
and then starting on the first one.
- Mark Twain

Darci Dawn

Do you generally feel respected as a woman?
Yes. As a broadcaster, I never play the stupid angle. I am always myself. I read people easily and know when to be "respectable" and know when I can be outrageous. (Laughing!)

What is your own personal definition of "respect"?
I feel respected when I'm understood, believed in and when I'm heard without judgment.

What did you do differently than most women to get where you are?
My background is in acting and when I went for auditions I understood clearly that it wasn't about competition at all, because we are all individuals. If they wanted me, they would offer the part to me.

One thing that I think I did differently to get where I am was to be very aggressive and used my charming sarcasm. I'm 100% "What you see is what you get." I think that many people put on faces to get the job that they want. I didn't. Some think that I'm too honest, but that is who I am. I'm still learning about business. Sometimes you don't say EVERYTHING to be a good businesswoman and apparently, that still equates to telling the truth

Was respect something you had to consciously work to achieve?
No. It is a given. Those who do not offer respect to others do not command it for themselves.

Are the factors that create respect at work the same factors as those that create respect at home?

Yes, and respect is especially important when you are raising kids. I am the same person I am at work as I am at home. I'm a compassionate, emotional, creative, and honest individual and I'm lucky that the job I have allows me to be who I am (to a degree).

What would you advise women to do to be taken seriously – by men and women?

♀ Be confident.

♀ Know yourself, faults and strengths – accepting all of it.

♀ If you don't regard yourself well why should anyone else?

WOW!
Words of Wisdom

Don't be afraid to do what you love, that makes you happy and never lower your standards to please others.

Darci Dawn is my radio name. My real name is Anny Marr. I'm an actor before I'm a radio personality, with a background in sketch comedy and voice over. I graduated from Second City in Los Angeles.

I graduated with a Bachelor of Arts in Psychology at Cal State University Long Beach. I was an only child, born on the west coast in Los Angeles, November 26th, 1967, but soon moved to the east coast.

When I was a baby, my mother was diagnosed with myastenia gravis; a neuro-muscular disease. My father wasn't very

present in my life, and still isn't. So I bounced around from family member to family member, until we ended up in San Diego in 1976. I was interested in acting and performing at a very young age and involved myself in a local theater group.

When I got to college I decided that I needed to have a "real career," so that's why I graduated with a degree in Psychology. Once I left college I realized that I had to make my dreams come true, so I moved to LA to do so. That's what began my fabulous career in bartending; I liked to call myself a "mixologist."

I've appeared in several small budget films, some big budget films, and television. For films credits, please refer to my resume. When I was a kid, I would create what I would call, "Spooky Stories on Tape." I would make up my own story and (fully) add sound effects in the garage and I would play them from friends and family. I always loved to be in front of the mic. Oddly enough, when I was bartending one night in Los Angeles, a gentlemen walked up to me and said, "You're pretty quirky and pretty much a wise acre, how would you like to be in radio?" I didn't think he was serious, and I said, "Would you like a Tangaray and Tonic and extra limes, Mr. High Maintenance?" I took his card, called him and I got my interview on a Friday. By Monday, I was hired. That "High Maintenance" man is now my boss, and he's great. I've been in radio almost a year here in Bakersfield, CA, market 87. For those people that don't know, there are 283 markets that are rated, 87 wasn't a bad place to start; much less the morning drive.

I enjoy people. I get to use all my natural talents. I live in the happy little town of Bakersfield, CA with a modest population of 250,000, with my boyfriend Matthew, my cats, Paco and Luna and my ferret, Dudley.

Rita de Maintenon

Do you generally feel respected as a woman?
Yes. It was a process; as my self-respect and self-confidence improved the respect given by others grew as well.

What is your own personal definition of "respect"?
Treat others as you want to be treated without preconceived judgments. Remain open-minded and treat others as persons of value, one of God's children, who are worth the time and effort. You'll receive the same in return.

What did you do differently than most women to get where you are?
I respected the integrity of others and their value systems. I turn all challenges into learning opportunities. I ask myself, "How can I make this into a positive situation?" I believe everyone is entitled to a second chance and be treated respectfully. I always stay positive and quickly get past negative attitudes.

Was respect something you had to consciously work to achieve?
Yes, I started out with very little self-respect. Once I personally found my own self-worth at home, with the help of my husband, it became easier to expect *and accept* respect other places and with other people.

Are the factors that create respect at work the same factors as those that create respect at home?
Yes, I believe that the same approach to another person works at home and at work or, to put it into different words, I treated my husband with the same respect and feeling of equality as I did my bosses or my students.

Anybody that acts more important or smarter than the rest of the world really turns me off and it is clearly a show of insecurity. That, of course, comes from my background, I grew up with people who were manipulative and threw their weight and positions around to manipulate other people and the environment around them. They were wonderful teachers and I am grateful to them! My second husband was a very secure person and brought out the best in me, activating what I knew all along.

Some women are treated badly at home and are very successful at work, but I think it all comes from the inside. We must be able to say to others, "This is not acceptable." We must have guidelines and find ways to work through challenges and problems at work or at home.

What would you advise women to do to be taken seriously – by men and women?

♀ Professional women need to look, act, and dress like a professional women at all times. Better yourself wherever you are -- there is always room for improvement. Study, read and learn so that you can have intelligent conversations. Be compassionate and understanding to everyone.

♀ Use basic commonsense! Set your own personal boundaries: have safe sex, demonstrate integrity, speak out for yourself, value yourself, don't put up with abuse. It's all interconnected. Remember, if you don't like a situation, you can make changes.

WOW!

Words of Wisdom

It is all right to have a dream and that is the first step to making it come true.

Rita de Maintenon: Personally: My husband passed away two years ago and that allows me to direct even more energy towards my teaching and volunteer projects. Since he died I also started another business that was started from my passion of fiber arts: Heirloom Treasures gives me the opportunity to design and create Victorian Needle Arts. I specialize in baby items, Christening outfits, carriage covers etc. I have 2 stepchildren, grandchildren in California and Florida and I live with 2 fat cats in a log house we built from scratch.

I was born, an only child, August 1, in Frankfurt, Germany just after World War II. My family was Catholic, strict to the point of being abusive; my father had an important position with the City and I was privileged, private school, cotillion, travels etc. but no personal freedom, it was their way or no way. I spoke English, Spanish and some French and Italian by the time I was 14. My first marriage lasted 12 years and took me to Texas and Florida where I met my second husband and we moved to NC together after he retired in Florida.

Professionally: Since 1992 Rita instructed and consulted for Southwestern Community College. She teaches Adult Basic Education, Special Education, Conversa-tional German and Fiber Arts and acts as an Industrial Development Consultant on the Business and Industry Training Team.

Rita is experienced in teaching, supervising, managing and program coordination on an international, national and local level. Her career spans teaching exceptional children's programs, managing multi-million dollar national accounts for several major U.S. Corporations, and independent business owner and manager of a manufacturing and maintenance corporation, which served the NASA shuttle program and other prestigious hydraulic and pneumatic equipment customers.

As a proactive citizen for increased quality of life in Macon County, Rita coordinated the Macon Senior Leadership Programs for Southwestern Community College and is involved with several non-profit organizations. She currently serves on the board of Macon Partners for a Healthy Future and the Macon County Community Foundation.

Rita holds a degree in Special Education with a minor in Physical Education and Physical Therapy.

"Three things in human life are important.
The first is to be kind.
The second is to be kind.
And the third is to be kind.
Harry James

Tami DePalma

Do you generally feel respected as a woman?
Yes, I don't feel discriminated against.

What is your definition of "respect"?
It all starts with self. Those who will don't feel respected are mirroring a lack of self-respect. Ask yourself, "Is this is my problem and do I need to be here?"

What did you do differently than most women to get where you are?
I would recommend my path. I follow whims and I follow my intuition. I keep going until I make it happen. (Laughing!) If you always follow your head, you're not honoring your heart. Find a way to honor your heart.

Was respect something you had to consciously work to achieve?
I don't think so.

Are the factors that create respect at work the same as those that create respect at home?
I believe so. If you're leading a life of duality, the incongruity will get to you some time and work or home will suffer.

What would you advise women to do to be taken seriously – by men and women?
♀ Do what you know you can do. Don't back down when they tell you you're crazy. … and they will.
♀ Take advice judiciously. Just because someone's older, or more experienced, doesn't mean they know more than you about you and your life.

♀ Live in respect with yourself.

Words of Wisdom

Self-care choices might make you feel selfish, but if you don't take care of *you*, you can't take care of others.

Tami DePalma: Tami is a Body-for-LIFE Champion, partner at *MarketAbility*, www.marketability.com, author of *MAXIMUM EXPOSURE Marketing System*, and delivers the powerful publicity presentation *The Missing 5th P --Four Easy Steps that Build Profit from Your Publicity*.

Her photo has graced the front cover of *Woman's World Magazine*, and she has gotten her clients more than $750 million in media coverage, including *The Today Show, The Jenny Jones Show, Live with Regis, USA Today, New York Times, LA Times, Washington Post, Chicago Tribune, Wall Street Journal, Investor's Business Daily, US News and World Report, Woman's Day, Cosmo, Glamour, Parents, Entrepreneur, Inc.*, they've booked over 3,000 radio interviews.

She has a background in all facets of marketing: advertising, merchandising, promotion, sales and customer service, and of course PR. Tami received her bachelor's of science in business administration with a concentration in marketing from Colorado State University. In 1993, she founded *YOU & MEdia Public Relations*, and soon merged with *MarketAbility*, to provide full-service marketing. Together with her "other better business half" Kim they have fine-tuned their business into book marketing.

She's featured in *The Body-for-LIFE Success Journal, How to Build Your Body-for-LIFE Video, Body-for-LIFE Cookbook.* She's writing several books on personal and professional success, the next to come out is *5 Pillars of Wellness.*

Married to Gino DePalma for 11 years. No kids yet, just 3 nephews Jake, Ben, Ross, and a niece, Tasmyn, Cat named Iniki. and Dogs Rasta (Lab-Collie) and Prints (Dalmatian).

I was born October 25, 1968, in New Jersey, moved to Colorado when I was a toddler, have lived here all my life. Arvada is a northwest suburb of Denver, halfway between Denver and Boulder. I'm the baby of three sisters who still wish we were Charlie's Angels!

"Our life is what our thoughts make it."
Marcus Aurelius Antonius

Susan Diamond

Do you generally feel respected as a woman?
Yes, I've never had a problem. However, when I started off in the family business, gender was a barrier to respect within the family. (Laughing!)

What is your own personal definition of "respect"?
I feel respected when my input is taken seriously and I am considered a competent professional.

What did you do differently than most women to get where you are?
I devoted a full-time schedule to my work. Some women try to succeed on a part-time basis and that is difficult.

I continued to search for career opportunities and business opportunities that kept me happy and intellectually stimulated and challenged.

Was respect something you had to consciously work to achieve?
No. I have a confident and professional demeanor and a strong business presence.

Are the factors that create respect at work the same factors as those that create respect at home?
No. The strength and confidence that I exude in business would be intimidating in a family setting.

What would you advise women to do to be taken seriously – by men and women?

♀ Place yourself in a situation where you can develop expertise and have passion about what you do. That passion will come through and respect is a logical by-product.

♀ Avoid any career for which you are ill suited. Trial and error is not a bad thing – you just might bump into your life's purpose.

WOW!

Words of Wisdom

Juggling work and family are difficult. Do all you can do to focus on one at a time.

Susan Diamond is a recognized leader in the field of sales and marketing consulting. Ms. Diamond's keen industry insight is attributable to her 20 years of professional cross-industry experience working with sales and marketing business process methodology as a salesperson, marketing representative, manager and business owner. From her multi-faceted background, she offers a unique perspective that embraces technology while utilizing common sense practices to enhance marketing and sales productivity.

In 1985 Ms. Diamond founded *Gold Coast Bows Inc.,* a textile manufacturing business specializing in the production and sale of children's accessories to the retail market. Five years later, this profitable company was sold and its founder was on her way to new challenges.

Ms. Diamond continued her successful business career by forming a contracting company located in the Jefferson Park

area of Chicago, Illinois. Serving consumers throughout the city, **Diamond Home Products Inc.** was a sales organization focusing on providing quality home remodeling at affordable pricing. Ms. Diamond soon affiliated with **Sears Roebuck and Company** as an authorized licensed contractor. Ms. Diamond's unique style of marketing, sales and personnel management programs were brought to the attention of Arthur Martinez, chairman of the board of **Sears Roebuck and Company** and his management team. Ms. Diamond received an **Excellence in Business Development** award for her efforts and a request to implement her effective strategies within the organization to other licensees. It was at this time that Ms. Diamond began her present career, serving as a resource to other companies for sales and marketing productivity.

In her role as managing partner for **White Diamond Consulting Group**, Ms. Diamond is delighted to be able to consistently help her clients achieve their marketing and sales goals through the successful integration of technologies into sound business practices. **wwwWhiteDiamondConsultings.com**

Education, Association Affiliations: University of Illinois, *International Association of Sales Process Consultants, American Marketing Association, NAWBO – National Association of Women's Business Owners, Association of Professional Management Consultants, International Business Analysts*

Married to husband David a partner in a C.P.A. firm located in Schaumburg. 4 children; Craig (soon to be married to Shani,) Howie, Michael and Rachel. Lived in the Chicago, Illinois area (Skokie then Northbrook) all my life, I'm 46 years old.

Dr. M. Tina Dupree,
The Chicken Lady

Do you generally feel respected as a woman?
Most of the time. I present myself in such a way that says, "I am to be respected." My father was a great role model and I learned from him about love, trust, and respect. He taught me that I deserved the best at all times. But in order to get it, I first had to respect myself and then others would respect me.

What is your own personal definition of "respect"?
You earn the credit that is given to you. Whenever you give respect to others, you earn the respect that is given to you. It is reciprocal. We should carefully consider how we treat others. So my definition would be that respect is the credit that you earn by the manner in which you have respected others.

What did you do differently than most women to get where you are?
I started as a maid, scrubbing floors. The woman whom I worked for (Carol) built my confidence and told me I could do more with my life. I tell the story in my book, *It's Time to Invest in Yourself*, how she came home one day and told me that because the Civil Rights Bill had been passed, I no longer had to scrub floors. (Laughing!) She opened up a door of opportunity that I never knew existed simply because she believed in me. This started me on the road to success.

There have been so many others who believed in me and helped me along the way, mostly men, who either challenged me by recognizing my talents or tried to make me fail by trying to block my success. But I was persistent and I would not

give up. Failing was not an option. I wanted success to live a life that I only dreamed of those days when I worked as a maid. I knew that there was more for me and many people helped me achieve the success that I have today. I am very grateful.

Was respect something you had to consciously work to achieve?
Respect was something that I always wanted. I respected others and I wanted it for myself. I wanted to earn the trust and respect that I saw that people had for my father. I worked harder than anyone else on every job that I have ever had. Even on jobs that I did not like or was not treated fairly. And I was respected for it. As I said before, you have to earn respect. This is not always easy but it can be accomplished.

Are the factors that create respect at work the same factors as those that create respect at home?
Yes, most definitely. The home sets precedent for how you behave at work. At home, you are really who you are-- just more relaxed. (Laughing!) At work you should be the same. It's hard trying to wear two faces.

What would you advise women to do to be taken seriously – by men and women?
Be real! -- not someone else. When they meet you, let it be the real you. Be consistent in everything that you do.

Never for a moment believe that everyone is on your side, but *act* as though they are. Persistence is the key, never give up trying and don't doubt yourself. You can do anything your heart desires. It just takes a little longer sometimes.

In my book, *It's Time To Invest In Yourself*, I advise people to find out what you really want and then move forward from

there. Most women don't live in their true potential because they get discouraged and either give up or give in. But I believe in standing and when I am pushed down, I get up and start all over again. Nothing can stop you if you believe in yourself.

Dr. Tina Dupree is lovingly known internationally as The Chicken Lady, **www.thechickenlady.com,** because of 12 years experience as the spokesperson for a major fast food chicken restaurant chain. When she resigned from her corporate level position with them to start the Motivational Training Center, the corporation contracted her as their community spokesperson. As the owner of the Motivational Training Center she presents personal and professional development interactive keynote speeches, corporate training programs, and monthly seminars on Public Speaking, Professional Speaking, Customer Service, Leadership, and Training Trainers to Train.

Dr. Dupree has authored three books and she is currently working on her new book, *Room to Grow: The Doorway to achieving your True POTENTIAL!* She is a Professional Member of the *National Speakers Association* (NSA), and is currently NSA's Liaison for the Chapters in the State of Florida.

Dr. Dupree served as the 1999-2000 President of the Florida Speakers Association, and is the radio talk show host for Building Bridges on WMCU 89.7 FM in Miami and 101.9 in Palm Beach. In 2001 she received a special invitation by

President George W. Bush to the White House for a special discussion on reforming education. As Founder of a non-profit organization, *Professional Speakers Network, Inc.*, she has personally trained and certified more than 150 speakers. Forty-three of them as a result of their training have written and published their own books.

She has a Bachelor of Science degree from Trinity International University, Master of Science degree from Jacksonville Theological Seminary and a Doctorate degree from Jacksonville Theological Seminary. Tina is the mother of two and the grandmother of five. Born November 4, a middle child, in Manning, South Carolina - grew up in Miami, Florida.

I find it fascinating that most people
plan their vacations with better care
than they plan their lives.
Perhaps that is because
escape is easier than change.
- Jim Rohn

Rita Emmett

Do you generally feel respected as a woman?
Now I do. I'm a professional speaker and author. Women speakers and authors are respected. I don't think I felt respected as a younger woman, but I didn't respect myself at that time. I went into therapy to work through the feelings associated with a divorce, and stayed to work through some personal issues. Then I dealt with self-respect issues.

At that time, I was presenting classes on assertiveness, and my therapist said, "Rita, do you ever listen to what that wonderful assertiveness teacher teaches?" I was teaching it but that I wasn't living it. (Laughing!)

What is your own personal definition of "respect"?
Being worthy and deserving of high regard, esteem or consideration.

What did you do differently than most women to get where you are?
I work hard. I'm good at figuring out where I want to go, setting goals, making a plan and going after it. It wasn't always that way. I used to spend a lot of time concerned with what I did not want. I've learned to focus on what I do want, to spend time dreaming about it, to talk to people I admire about it, and keep my eyes open for opportunities for it to happen. Also, I've always had a standard of excellence, and try to choose the ethical, right path.

Was respect something you had to consciously work to achieve?

Yes, everyone else's needs, wants, and projects all were far more important to me than my own. I found that once I truly respected myself, respect from others just came automatically.

Are the factors that create respect at work the same as those that create respect at home?
They're basically the same. You have to learn what you are willing to put up with and what you will not tolerate.

What would you advise women to do to be taken seriously – by men and women?
Eleanor Roosevelt said, "No one can make you feel inferior without your consent." At work and at home, we have to teach others how we expect to be treated. If we use words such as "I'm *just* an administrative assistant" or "I may not know what I'm talking about but I think ..." others hear us negate ourselves, and they believe us.

However, if you have done your part and you know you're worthy of respect and you're still not getting it, you may need to change your environment. I divorced and changed careers.

Why is it more respectable to watch football than to watch soap operas? Women will patiently listen while men discuss football games on Monday morning, but no one will patiently listen while women discuss soap operas. *Neither men nor women.* Soap operas are belittled while football games are worthy of discussion. Why is that?

Rita Emmett is a professional speaker, President of Emmett Enterprises, Inc. since 1985, and author of the best seller *THE PROCRASTINATOR'S HANDBOOK: Mastering the Art of*

Doing It Now, and *THE PROCRASTINATING CHILD: A Handbook for Adults to Help Children Stop Putting Things Off.* **www,RitaEmmett.com**

Rita, who lives in Des Plaines, Illinois, has been honored for her High Content / High Fun interactive Keynotes and Training presentations by being included in the prestigious *"Who's Who in American Education"* plus *"Who's Who in America"* and the *"The World Wide Who's Who of Women."* Also, she has been the Keynote Speaker at the Governor's Mansion in Springfield, Illinois. Some of Rita's clients include AT&T, Kraft Food, Mercedes Benz, Met Life, and The National Kidney Foundation.

Rita earned her MS in Adult Learning at National Lewis University.

She is married to Bruce Karder whom she met in the cat food aisle at the grocery store, and together they have a blended family of 5 kids, 4 kids-in-law and 9 glorious, gorgeous, smart, talented grandchildren.

Birth date April 12, in Chicago, grew up in Chicago and Franklin Park, IL. One brother, seven years older

"Make your decisions principle-driven so you do what is most important to you at the time.
-- David DArcangelo

Patricia Ferguson

Do you generally feel respected as a woman?
YES, I feel respected for my intellectual capital, for my commitment to making meaningful differences in the communities I serve and males usually accept me.

What is your own personal definition of "respect"?
To appreciate the differences among us and the freedom to disagree.

What did you do differently than most women to get where you are?
Eliminated barriers to success that existed in my own mind because of cultural norms, or because of the way women are portrayed in the media and the broader community. In my world I eliminated the glass ceiling, celebrated my victories AND my "lessons learned." On a daily basis I evaluated my performance and recommended to myself an improvement plan. I was willing to face my shortcomings and call them *growth points*, (Laughing!) and EXPECTED that I would make the needed adjustments to put me back on course to fulfilling my mission.

Was respect something you had to consciously work to achieve?
No. It began with ME respecting myself first, and others "catching it" and doing the same.

Are the factors that create respect at work the same factors as those that create respect at home?
Yes, basically they are. I'm not sure how you change them. At work there must be consistency of what you value and the same can be said for home. What you value becomes threaded into everything you do.

Create your own personal "work" and "family" constitutions which can be invaluable tools used to express the worth of relationships, and how its significance translates into the work that has to take place if co-workers or family members' goals are to be realized.

What would you advise women to do to be taken seriously – by men and women?

♀ Be sure of yourself and never be afraid of detours.
♀ Make up your own mind after conversations with "trusted" advisors
♀ Never blame your shortcomings on others.
♀ Celebrate victories as well as lessons learned!
♀ Learn to learn from everyone. — be no "respecter of persons" and treat all equally.
♀ Encourage yourself as often as needed
♀ Smile always! Speak good things and think good thoughts and pray without ceasing.

Never let the sun go down on your wrath---forgive as often as needed!

Patricia Ferguson
Masters in Education, NC County Commissioner
Former Senate Candidate, Born and grew up in North Carolina, I am the mother of two boys.

Marilyn D. Fitzgerald

Do you generally feel respected as a woman?
Yes.

What is your own personal definition of "respect"?
I feel respected when others honor and support what I do.

What did you do differently than most women to get where you are?
I didn't really do much differently. My mother was a good role model for me to follow and provided a sound foundation for me as an entrepreneur. She made decisions, pursued and achieved her goals. Men were not required. She just decided what she wanted and went for it.

Was respect something you had to consciously work to achieve?
All people need to work for respect. I've often worked in male-dominated fields. I gave respect by honoring them and their knowledge and working as hard as I knew how. That earned their respect.

Are the factors that create respect at work the same factors as those that create respect at home?
Yes, and it's all based on trust, which is the foundation for respect.

What would you advise women to do to be taken seriously – by men and women?
Identify your strengths. Understand and improve your level of self-esteem. If there is anything that makes you feel less than complete, deal with it until you feel good about yourself.

WOW!
Words of Wisdom

The only person stopping you from attaining what you want is YOU.

Marilyn D. Fitzgerald is a nationally known keynote presenter, trainer and consultant. She is a former co-host of the Les Brown Show on WYPA Personal Achievement Radio Station. Marilyn was groomed for the business world since in childhood with involvement in her family's business ventures. She has been a seasoned entrepreneur and sales leader for over a decade. Marilyn has innate marketing, production management, and operational design knowledge in multiple industries, including retail and restaurant operations.

As the president of Mystic Enterprises Inc., Marilyn served as consultant to Kraft General Foods, Brach Candy Company, Coca-Cola, Oprah Winfrey's Harpo Studio and the Four Seasons Hotel. General Motors awarded her their prestigious Minority of the Year award.

As the president of Marilyn D. Fitzgerald Communications, Inc., she presents programs nationally for her company and several seminar-leading companies. She speaks on empowerment and human resources. Some of Marilyn's satisfied clients include Harvard Business School, Chi - Chi's Restaurants, African American Women on Tour, Old Kent Mortgage Company, Upjohn Pharmaceutical Company, General Service Administration and Naval Control Point. Marilyn has made several appearances and interviews on TV and radio, including WGN Television, Talking Success and WYAA, WYCA and WYCC radio stations.

Patricia Fripp, CSP, CPAE

Do you generally feel respected as a woman?
Yes. Of course I communicate differently in different circumstances. When I was a hairstylist at age 23, I would **TELL** executives how to wear their hair. I would tell them what and I would tell them why, and they would never argue. It has only gotten better.

What is your own personal definition of "respect"?
If they ask for and pay for your advice, they take it! (Laughing!)

I feel respected when I'm listened to and people pay attention to my advice and I return the favor. I am also very aware of visible signals of communication.

What did you do differently than most women to get where you are?
Well, I'm a compulsive overachiever. I left school before I was 15 so I'm not traditionally well educated – I only go to college when I lecture there. (Laughing!) I knew at a very young age that I wanted to stay single. I like to work and I like to be independent.

When I heard executives talking about their lives, *I wanted their life,* not the life of their wives. It seemed to me to be more sensible to become an executive than to marry one.

Was respect something you had to consciously work to achieve?
Never even thought about it!

Are the factors that create respect at work the same factors as those that create respect at home?
No idea! I would think so. I have no spouse or kids. I do have personal relationships with men but I don't have to deal with

them on a daily basis. (Laughing!) I am amazed at the women who balance it all because it takes a lot of time and energy.

What advice would you give women to help them get taken seriously – by men and women?

♀ Learn to communicate more effectively

♀ Dress well, stand tall, and walk with authority.

♀ You may have to be twice as good as a man to get the same results and if that's what it takes, do it! Results don't lie.

♀ You get what you focus on.

♀ It is not who you know, but who wants to know you.

You have to make life choices. Dru Scott said, "After being single for years, I married and inherited children and I am embarrassed to admit that I have told women they could do it all."

Patricia Fripp: Single, never married by choice. Born April 18, 1945, in the south of England, Wimborne Dorset. One brother, Robert, internationally acclaimed guitarist

Patricia Fripp, CSP, CPAE is an award-winning speaker, author, sales trainer and in-demand speech coach. Her speech-coaching clients include corporate leaders, celebrity speakers, well-known sports and media personalities, ministers, and sales teams. Meetings and Conventions magazine named her "One of the 10 most electrifying speakers in North America." She delivers high-energy, high-content, and dramatically memorable presentations. Steven Covey's Executive Excellence magazine named her "One of the top 50 consultants,

trainers, speakers, authors and professors who cover the Seven Dimensions of Excellence."

Before becoming a full-time speaker, Patricia enjoyed a successful career in a service industry for 24 years. She owned two highly successful businesses that included training both service and sales personnel.

Patricia first received payment for speaking and training in 1976. Since 1980 she has spoken to at least 100 groups a year, many of them repeat engagements. This includes Fortune 100 companies and major associations worldwide. The over 4,000-member National Speakers Association elected her the first female President in 1984. She has won or been awarded every designation given by NSA, including the Hall of Fame and the Cavett Award, the highest honor and considered the Oscar of the speaking world.

Patricia is the author of two books, *Get What You Want!* and *Make It, So You Don't Have to Fake It!*, and coauthor of *Speaking Secrets of the Masters* and *Insights into Excellence*. She is featured in the Bullet Proof Manager video series, which is sold in over fifty countries. Fripp starred in the popular training film *Travel the Road to Success: An Adventure in Customer Service.* **www.fripp.com**

There are only two ways to live your life.
One is as though nothing is a miracle.
The other is as though everything is a miracle.
-Albert Einstein

Patti Hathaway, CSP

Do you generally feel respected as a woman?
Yes.

What is your own personal definition of "respect"?
I feel respected when my opinion is valued and followed by others.

What did you do differently than most women to get where you are?
I've always been focused on goals. I was determined, self-directed, self-motivated and I went for it! I surround myself with people who encourage me. Example: I've always worked from my home and when I started having children, I had to learn to do things in small increments of time. As a result, I can get an incredible amount of work completed in a short period of time.

This has become a huge point of advantage for me. I've never focused on what I couldn't do but instead focused on what I *could* do. I rarely doubt myself and take more risks than most people. I "fake it till I make it" and usually make it as a result because I don't think otherwise!

Was respect something you had to consciously work to achieve?
Not consciously. I was a high school athlete and I understood the no pain – no gain principal. I've been described as driven and I'm very willing to take risks. Looking back, all of that gets you respect fairly easily. Admittedly, being six feet tall as a woman naturally garners respect merely by the fact that most people have to look up at me. (Laughing!)

Are the factors that create respect at work the same factors as those that create respect at home?
I think so, but getting respect at home is more challenging. Frankly, getting respect is easier at work. When people don't know you on a very deep level, it's easier to fake it when you need to. At home they know all of me, including vulnerabilities.

What would you advise women to do to be taken seriously – by men and women?
♀ Believe in yourself and take more risks.
♀ Act confident until you are confident.
♀ Be optimistic.
♀ Surround yourself with encouraging and successful people who challenge you and push you to be best you can.
♀ Cherish your primary relationships -- they're worth the work and will last beyond your work.

Don't forget that your children will ultimately be your greatest gift to this world. Keep that in mind in the midst of your professional flurry and desire to achieve success in the eyes of the world.

Patti Hathaway, CSP, The CHANGE AGENT, is one of fewer than 160 women worldwide to have earned the Certified Speaking Professional designation from the *National Speakers Association* for her proven presentation skills.
- Author of 4 books, which have been translated into 5 languages and have sold over 100,000 copies.

- Patti works with organizations that want to make change work and with those organizations that want to change their

customer service culture. She provides highly customized keynotes and workshops.

- For information on her speaking and consulting services or to receive her free e-mail newsletter, contact Patti at 1-800-339-0973 or at her web-sites: **www.thechangeagent.com** and **www.bankingsecrets.com**

- Age 43 (February 2 birthday), married to her husband and business partner Jim for 20 years (also a Feb. birthday) Two sons, Bryan (13) and Drew (10), 2 year old Bichon Frise dog, Sparky, who is a certified therapy dog. Born and grew up in Grand Rapids, Michigan where she graduated from Calvin College. She has 2 older sisters and a younger brother. Came to Columbus, Ohio to attend and earn her Masters degree from The Ohio State University. Patti and Jim have chosen to live in the Central Ohio area ever since.

Every person,
all the events of your life are there
because you have drawn them there.
- Richard David Bach

Susan B. Hirschmann

Do you generally feel respected as a woman?
Yes, as a person. Men never think of their accomplishments as gender-specific and I don't think women should have to either.

What is your own personal definition of "respect"?
Respect means people take your ideas seriously.

What did you do differently than most women to get where you are?
I prioritized my career in a very focused way. For example, I am 39 years old and I have no children because I've spent the time on my career. I have never figured out how to balance both. And of course, hard work and trying to always *do more than needed* is important to me.

Was respect something you had to consciously work to achieve?
Initially in politics I was underestimated as a very young female. I've used that to my advantage. (Laughing!)

Are the factors that create respect at work the same factors as those that create respect at home? Some are, some are not. Being organized, communicating well, multi-tasking, working hard can be applied both places. Sometimes women don't have the confidence in the work place to understand the value of these skills.

What would you advise women to do to be taken seriously – by men and women?
♀ Work hard; don't whine.

♀ Don't be afraid to present your ideas with authority.

♀ Have short-term and long-term plans and find ways to constantly measure your progress or you'll work hard with limited results.

Find a supportive group of strong women, who are confident, knowledgeable, and very secure. They can be invaluable.

Susan Brackin Hirschmann joined Williams & Jensen in 2002 as a "partner member." Susan provides strategic advice concerning the House and Senate and their Leadership as well as the Administration, as well as grassroots organizations.

From 1997 through 2002, Susan served as Chief of Staff to Tom DeLay (R-TX), Majority Whip of the House of Representatives. As his Chief of Staff her responsibilities included managing Rep. DeLay's personal, district and Whip offices. Susan also worked with the House and Senate Leadership to develop and execute Republican priorities. She worked with the Administration and other Members of Congress, their staffs, outside organizations, and businesses to pass legislation. Susan was named one of the top Hill staffers by the *National Journal* and was referred to as "one of Capitol Hills most influential Chiefs of Staff by *Roll Call,* and was recognized by the *National Journal* as one of the 100 Most Powerful Women in Washington, D.C. *The Washington Post* referred to Susan as "one of the most highly regarded staffers on Capitol Hill."

Before joining the Whip office, Susan was the Chief of Staff for Congressman Van Hilleary (R-TN) and prior to that, was

the executive director of Eagle Forum, a pro-family, national grassroots organization. At Eagle Forum, she lobbied Members of Congress and activated volunteers on issues. She also managed the organization's Political Action Committee, developed the direct mail and large donor fundraising program, trained volunteers and made media appearances for the organization.

Susan moved to Washington, D.C. in 1987 to run the College Republican National Committee. As executive director, she organized the college political efforts for the 1988 campaigns. She recently served as a visiting Fellow at Harvard University's John F. Kennedy Institute of Politics. She has her MS in Speech Pathology.

Deep within humans dwell
those slumbering powers;
powers that would astonish them,
that they never dreamed of possessing;
forces that would revolutionize their lives
if aroused and put into action.
-Orison Marden

Michele Bullis Hubbs

Do you generally feel respected as a woman?
I feel very respected. Occasionally, some individuals are not as open to women, but I have never felt "held back."

What is your own personal definition of "respect"?
That my thoughts can be my own to share or to keep. When you're approachable, others respect you. It's reciprocal - when you respect others, you get it back. It's very respectful to appreciate the differences and diversity of other people.

What did you do differently than most women to get where you are?
I've been a risk taker, and I've initiated changes. I am very adaptable. Many people choose to be "plankton on the sea of life." I choose to be the current and have made the choice to change careers or location on several occasions.

Was respect something you had to consciously work to achieve?
No, I respected myself through good and bad. I have a strong, grounded background. And my mother said that happiness is always a daily choice. I believe that.

Are the factors that create respect at work the same factors as those that create respect at home?
Respect is a little harder to achieve out of the home. I get respect in the workplace but I see many women having difficulty because they are insecure.

What would you advise women to do to be taken seriously – by men and women?

♀ Be a pleasant person and people will be more open to your ideas. Like yourself and like other people.

♀ When you smile and genuinely like people and they feel warmth from you, they feel respect for you.

♀ Have the backbone to be self-sufficient, but appreciate opportunities to share the load!

♀ Have faith.

♀ Self-respect and self-esteem are essential.

♀ Being a victim is not a good role for anyone...nobody likes a whiner!

Words of Wisdom

Perfection is overrated. Don't try to be perfect and don't beat yourself up when you're not. Keep things in perspective; a Bad Hair Day will not ruin the rest of your life. (*Laughing!*)

Michele Hubbs: Born Michele Snow Bullis, I grew up a "corporate brat" as my dad was an executive with DuPont Company, with many moves in the Eastern U.S. My mom was a stay-home mom, and with my two brothers were a very close family. Both parents have died of cancer but I still enjoy closeness with both brothers and my large extended family.

Born March 19, (The Day the Swallows Come Back to Capistrano) in 1952 in Orangeburg, SC. Grew up mostly in NC, and also SC, TN, VA, WVA, DE, KY, FL, in suburbs and small towns. I am the middle child of three, sandwiched in-between brothers Chris and Dean. Timothy Shawn Hubbs, Husband, Amanda Snow Thompson,

Daughter (23), Angela and Noah Hubbs, Stepchildren (22 and 21), Houdini, Beloved Mutt (who adopted us seven years ago) Cardinals, Chickadees, Redheaded Woodpeckers, Beloved Wild Bird "Regulars"

Graduated HS in Wilmington, NC in 1970 and attended several colleges (USF and UK), before graduating from UNC at Wilmington in 1974 with a degree in Education.

Married and moved to Jacksonville, FL, taught school, had daughter, Amanda Snow Thompson in 1980. Got divorced, moved to Southeastern Pennsylvania later that year. Taught in private prep school for 6-7 years, left teaching to design jewelry and start jewelry line, Periwinkle Originals. Worked with own line as well as "repping" several other fashion and jewelry lines in wholesale buyers' markets in NYC, Philadelphia, Baltimore, and other Mid-Atlantic cities and on the road. Left the business to avoid too much time away from daughter.

Worked as Curator of Education and Public Relations at Brandywine Battlefield Park and Museum in Chadds Ford, Pa. for two years. Moved to Franklin, NC in the Smoky Mountains and went back to teaching in 1992. Currently teaching Science at Macon Middle School and one Saturday per month do Ecological Research for the Nat'l Science Foundation and U of Ga.

In 1998, after nearly twenty years single, married "love of my life," Timothy Shawn Hubbs, Executive VP of Drake Software. In addition to daughter, Mandy (23), have two stepchildren, Angela (22) and Noah (21). I am a Christian woman active in the Methodist Church. In addition to church activities, we attend hospital functions through Tim's membership on the hospital board. We both are

former Toastmasters and have just signed up for "Swing Dance" lessons.

Use what talent you possess:
the woods would be very silent
if no birds sang
except those that sang best.
-Henry Van Dyke

Catherine Johns

Do you generally feel respected as a woman?
Absolutely! 25 years ago I might have answered differently but it turns out that time has some positive implications as well as the negative ones we're all familiar with. (Laughing!) It's not so much about chronological age as it is about what that age suggests in terms of experience and wisdom -- those are the things that generate respect.

What is your own personal definition of "respect"?
It has to do with how people treat me, talk to me and talk about me.

What did you do differently than most women to get where you are?
I'm not sure my path was so different. Like others, I worked hard; I valued my relationships with both women and men in my radio career.   It may have helped that I was single for a long time -- because that allowed a single-minded focus on my work.

Was respect something you had to consciously work to achieve?
Yes. It was partly a timing issue. When I got into radio there were very few women on the air. They told me that women didn't belong on the air, that no one liked women's voices. I had to be very good to overcome that negativity about being female. I developed an essential edge early on because it was a boys' game.

My former (male) colleagues aren't likely to read a book about women and respect ... but if they did, I know they'd be amused to hear that quality being described as "an essential

edge." I suspect they'd have a different name for it! (Laughing!)

Are the factors that create respect at work the same factors as those that create respect at home?
Yes, probably. There are internal qualities to consider such as being ethical and intelligent, knowing your job, and treating people well that apply everywhere.

There are are also external qualities that count for a lot. You have to ask yourself: What do others see when they look at me and hear when they listen to me. Does my "look" generate respect? Do I carry myself proudly? Does my demeanor suggest authority? Credibility? Leadership?

What would you advise women to do to be taken seriously – by men and women?
If you don't know already, learn to project that air of authority and credibility. Look and sound like someone to be taken seriously. As business communication consultants, we work with clients to help them do just that. And ... be very good at what you do. Or at least be perceived as someone who's learning to be very good.

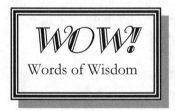

It's not so much what you say that makes an impression on people, it's how you say it. Work on the "how."

Catherine Johns: BA in Communications from Western Illinois University.

After years of turning my quest for Mr. Right into radio fodder ... I finally did find him! Frank and I will be married 12

years this summer. He's wonderful! Born 11/03/52 ... yes, it's hard to acknowledge the year. Who ever expects to be 50??? So far, it's turned out to be better than I expected. Don't feel a day over 49. (Laughter!)

Born in Ft. Wayne, Indiana. Dad was in the Army ... two grandmas were at the hospital with my mother. Grew up in Glenview, Illinois. Still spend time with Glenview friends from high school and even grade school. (It was shocking when they turned our elementary school into a senior citizens' center!)

One sister, one brother ... both younger. One way to get men to take you seriously is to start practicing early on those younger siblings.

Catherine Johns is a consultant with Rogen International Group in Chicago. Rogen specializes in persuasive communication and Catherine certainly has a lot of experience in persuasion! Her first career on the radio prepared her for working with clients in presentation skills, sales communication, facilitation, and of course media skills.

Midwesterners know Catherine from her years at WLS and Oldies 104.3; she was a talk show host, news anchor and morning show side-chick. Catherine brings that same flair for sparkling communication to her consulting and coaching.

Catherine is a certified NLP Practitioner and a yoga student. She lives in a northwest side bungalow with her husband Frank.

Carol Johnson

Do you generally feel respected as a woman?
Yes, I never felt that my gender hurt me.

What is your own personal definition of "respect"?
I feel respected when peers seek me out for career advice and value my opinion both personally and professionally.

What did you do differently than most women to get where you are?
My strongest attributes are creativity and my networking skills. I connect the dots because I think futuristically. Apparently I often think way ahead of the curve! (Laughing!) Many of my professional contacts have come to appreciate this skill and others never will.

Was respect something you had to consciously work to achieve?
No, you earn respect by doing what you should be doing, but doing it with the highest level of professionalism, enthusiasm and integrity. My high-pitched soft voice sometimes causes people to underestimate me. On the other hand, it also gives me an edge; because it tends to put me on a personal level with people much sooner.

If I were mentoring soft-spoken women, seeking employment in the corporate world, I would suggest they consider taking voice lessons to develop a more authoritative, modulated tone.

Are the factors that create respect at work the same factors as those that create respect at home?
I believe the skills are the same. You can't be one person at work and another at home. It's important to be fair, honest,

nurturing and to set parameters in both places. Well-developed relationship skills can be used in business, social or personal environments.

What would you advise women to do to be taken seriously – by men and women?
Become an expert on something. Study it in serious detail and identify where you can make a contribution. Have a firm grasp on who the leaders are and who you want to take you seriously. Don't hesitate to approach the experts in your field. Pick up the phone and call them or send a short email! If you have a compelling reason to talk to industry leaders, authors or political figures, they will give you the time.

There is an evolution of women and workplace.

Ages 50 plus believe it is OK to succeed. **30 to 50** are seeking with the balance. **Under 30?** Seek wisdom and humility. Learn from those who went before and you'll get there faster.

Carol Johnson is a noted authority on real estate recruiting and retention. She is the founder and President of the Recruiting Network and Publisher of the Recruiting Pipeline web site. The organization is the real estate industry's largest and most recognized resource for real estate related recruiting and HR information.

She is a consultant to emerging technology firms whose products and services impact recruiting and agent productivity systems. She hosts a series of public and private Tele-classes, and interviews leading recruiters, managers and authors about recruiting related matters. She coaches and advises real estate professionals on recruiting strategy including the development of on-line recruiting tools.

Her book, *The Recruiting Revolution in Real Estate* is credited with changing the way the real estate industry approaches recruiting. The Recruiting Network's web site, *www.RecruitingPipeline.com* serves as the hub of real estate recruiting information.

She is active in Toastmasters and involved in local and professional organizations. Her community and peers have recognized her with community and service awards including Realtor Associate of the Year for the State of Illinois.

Education: John Muir High Pasadena California, Pasadena City College, San Diego State University BS

Family: Married to David Johnson 39 years, 3 Kids James (Sue), Darrin (Kim) Dayna and 1 grand child. Pets: Two dogs Elmo and Muffin who serve as Vice Presidents of Recruiting Network Born on May 7 and raised in Pasadena/Altadena, California. One sister Sandie Wilson Smith.

Most people achieved their greatest successes
one step beyond
what looked like their greatest failure.
-Brian Tracy

Elyse Hope Killoran

Do you generally feel respected as a woman?
Yes, I do feel generally respected and I believe that that is a direct result of how I feel about myself.

What is your own personal definition of "respect"?
Respect between two people creates an equal playing field, a sense of appreciation and the opportunity to move beyond a hierarchical interaction.

What did you do differently than most women to get where you are?
I fell flat on my face at first; I found that it didn't hurt all that much, and I wasn't afraid to do it again. Before my evolutionary "growth spurt," whenever I would get out of my comfort zone I would pull back. Now I know that living on the edge equals growth. Women have traditionally chosen safety, harmony and comfort over growth. A friend of mine says he loves it when he gets uncomfortable because he knows that that is a signal that things are just about to get exciting!

Was respect something you had to consciously work to achieve?
My self-respect required work. I had to learn to be gentle with myself and more accepting and to learn that you get back what you put out.

Are the factors that create respect at work the same as those that create respect at home?
The dynamics are generally the same, however there is the added challenge that we expect those in our intimate circles

to be able to read our minds. At work we may personalize things less but find it more difficult to make our needs and wishes known so the pitfalls are the same in both areas.

What would you advise women to do to be taken seriously – by men and women?
My advice is always about bringing the most empowered you more to the surface.

Debbie Ford's work on shadows often provides people with significant breakthroughs. You might want to read: *The Dark Side of the Light Chasers: Reclaiming Your Power, Creativity, Brilliance and Dreams.*

I believe that everything we experience in our relationships with other people mirrors something that is going on inside of us. With my clients, instead of focusing on how they might get other people to change so that they might feel more comfortable, we bring attention to their own inner processes-- the beliefs, fears, emotional reactions that are keeping *recurring patterns* in place. By recognizing how we are (often unconsciously) contributing to our positive and negative experiences, we can become empowered to attract more of what we want and less of what we don't want.

The process of respect is inside-out work. It starts with   you in every relationship and expands outward. Progress that you make on one   level will have a domino effect in every area of you life. It is so worth it!

Elyse Hope Killoran, President of Prosperity from the Inside-Out, LTD., is a Personal Life Coach, the Founder of

Women's U. Virtual University, a LifePartnerQuest Relationship Coach and the Founder of The Prosperity Partnership.

Elyse graduated Phi Beta Kappa with Honors in Psychology from Franklin and Marshall College in Lancaster, PA. After a number of years in the educational field Elyse began her coach training at Coach U, continued at Coaching from Spirit and is a committed to continual skill enhancement through her lifetime membership in the Graduate School of Coaching.

You can read more about Elyse's professional development in the book *"Intentional Change: Personal and Professional Coaches Describe Their Work and Lives"* (on sale at amazon.com) and discover the intimate details of her personal quest at her web site http://www.spiritualpartnering.com. You can download her latest e-book *"Lessons from the Prosperity Game"* as a free gift from **www.projectprosperity.org**

Elyse is a single parent of two spirited sons (7 and 9) and the ringleader of a household that includes: one Lhasa Apso dog, one dwarf bunny and two Siamese fighting fish. Although they own separate homes, Elyse is dedicated to her relationship of three years with her spiritual partner John.

Born 6/18/65, Born in Brooklyn New York and grew up in Massapequa, Long Island. Eldest child of a single mom with one younger brother.

Our lives are shaped
not as much by our experience,
as by our expectations."
--- George Bernard Shaw

Connie Knutti

Do you generally feel respected as a woman?
Yes.

What is your own personal definition of "respect"?
Self-respect and confidence come first from within and then comes back to you from others.

What did you do differently than most women to get where you are?
My timing was good. I started out in the small town so I had more impact. I was honest and I was always prepared.

Was respect something you had to consciously work to achieve?
Lots of self-confidence brought respect. I'm told that I am low maintenance, not needy, and I did not challenge authority until I had built my muscles.

Are the factors that create respect at work the same factors as those that create respect at home?
Absolutely! Make good decisions at home and at work, choose wisely and be consistent.

What would you advise women to do to be taken seriously – by men and women?
♀ Don't let the competition dictate your focus.
♀ Laugh at yourself.

Balance all aspects of your life and don't let things get too out of kilter.

Connie Knutti: Married for 39 years, son 37, and daughter-in-law, daughter 32, and son-in-law, granddaughter 9, grandson 6, Mother 89, numerous aunts, uncles and cousins. I also count among my family, a very supportive group of friends. Born April 4, 1944 -- 04-04-44, Always a surprise to those who ask. Born in northwestern Illinois. Grew up in small town of less than 1,500 populations, typical of the 1950"s. One younger brother. My mom was 31 when I was born and 36 when my brother was born. My dad worked as a railroad engineer and my mom was, by the 1940's standards, an "OLD" stay-at-home mom.

Professionally:
State of Illinois - Department of Labor 1973- 2003
Manager of Field Enforcement, Chief Compliance Officer/Assistant Administrator , Compliance Officer - Assigned difficult cases throughout the state with broad and varying complaints. I supervise a field staff scattered all over the state. The fact that I was a woman drew more than a few challenges, but my willingness to share honestly with anyone who asks; politicians, citizens, employers, employees, staff, supervisors, attorneys, accountants, and counterparts throughout the country proved to be my best asset.

Education: Highland Community College. Attended multiple training sessions on: Computer programs, managing staff, labor relations seminars, human resource management, payroll and accounting practices

Memberships and Interests: Child Labor Committee Member of Interstate Labor Standards Association, Task Force Charter member of Chicago Area Workers Rights Initiative, Member of the former Illinois Education to Careers (School-to-Work) Steering Committee, Member of State Financial Literacy Committee, Trustee of Lanark Fire Protection District, Retired EMS volunteer,

Fledgling gardener

My formal speaking and leadership started in the 8th grade with the American Legion Good Citizen Award, then a nomination to mock government week known as Girls State. I represented my community, was active on campus, elected Chaplain of the Senate, gave the opening and closing prayers to hundreds without the slightest hesitation. The greatest fear of most people is public speaking but it never even occurred to me. I was elected president of my class and other various high school organizations gave talks and acted as the Master of Ceremonies on many occasions in both high school and post high school forums.

I entered state employment when women were just beginning to obtain key roles in both the public sector and private industries. EEOC, civil rights, and NOW were all active and just starting to make a difference in the working world. I first encountered wonderful women who were secretaries or payroll clerks but not human resource professionals, accountants, attorneys or CEO's. After thirty years, I am happy that some of that has changed.

I worked very hard, prepared myself mentally for any task, not wanting to be embarrassed or caught off guard by any lack of knowledge of the subject at hand. It was done as a matter of pride and for a sense of professionalism, not as a feminine challenge. If you have something to sell, focus on its merit, not on the weakness of others.

Dawn Bodo Lehman, Ph.D.

Do you generally feel respected as a woman?
Yes.

What is your own personal definition of "respect"?
To honor the opinions, perspectives, and beliefs of others even though you may not agree with them. To honor yourself as a creative, caring, spiritual being capable of reaching your highest potential.

What did you do differently than most women to get where you are?
I have never really differentiated myself from other women. I worked hard alongside my female co-workers in the automotive industry, which expected dedication and excellence from both men and women. I did not compete with others. I focused on developing my skills so that my managers would give me opportunities to try new things. The more I increased my skills, the greater the opportunities that came my way. I always challenged myself to be the best I could be.

I learned early in my career about the stereotypes that working mothers faced. Many men didn't quite believe that a woman could "pull her weight." Mothers, they thought, were too preoccupied with family matters to be completely committed to their job. I followed in the steps of other successful women who proved that we could succeed in both domains. To avoid perpetuating this stereotype, these women ONLY shared baby photos and discussed family issues with co-workers during the lunch break or after work.

Was respect something you had to consciously work to achieve?
Yes. Working in a male dominated field, I learned to speak to men very directly. I became more articulate as I presented facts, and I reduced emotion (I previously **loved** superlatives!) in my communications. (Laughing!)

I found that men were more likely to listen to, and act upon, my advice if I spoke their language. I did not ignore my feminine qualities; I just created balance in my communication style. I learned that communication outcomes depended on the way I responded to others. Conscious choices regarding communications styles resulted in respect from male co-workers during my 25-year career in the industry.

Are the factors that create respect at work the same factors as those that create respect at home?
Basically, yes, but it's not always the same at home. Family members don't always understand how hard you work in the workplace and at home, especially when your work takes time away from them. Multi-tasking is our way of life, and often we feel unappreciated for all that we do. On the other hand, many women receive more respect if they earn a good salary. Women who do not work outside the home are often undervalued because their work does not provide a financial reward.

What would you advise women to do to be taken seriously – by men and women?
- ♀ Be the very best that you can be. Compete only with yourself, show responsibility, and respect the opinions of others.
- ♀ Have courage to stand up for what you believe, but employ a communication style that matches that of the people to whom you are speaking.

♀ At home, stand strong in the face of expectations. Communicate the importance of family teamwork and responsibility. Both spouse and children will sense your presence of mind and will more likely respond positively and with respect.

♀ My personal philosophy is based on the late advertising genius, Leo Burnett: Reach for the stars in all that you do. You may not catch one, but you won't come up with a handful of mud, either.

♀ Keep a positive attitude, and try to create win-win results from every challenge you face.

♀ Honor and respect yourself and others will respect you, too.

♀ Help your sisters whenever you can. Never downgrade another woman in front of men, for that only perpetuates stereotypes, diminishes respect, and slows our concerted efforts to succeed in business.

WOW!

Words of Wisdom

Combine all of the knowledge, wisdom and experience of your mind, body and soul. Build on your strengths and know that God is always by your side in times of trouble.

Dawn Bodo Lehman received her doctoral degree in cultural anthropology from Wayne State University. She combines 25 years marketing communications experience with 13 years of NIH- and corporate-funded research in the areas of public health, business, corporate communications, and personal image. Her research helps businesses solve problems associated with customer satisfaction, employee satisfaction, internal and business-to-business communications, corporate restructuring, mergers, marketing, and the implementation of

new technology. Through funding from pharmaceutical companies and health coalitions, she has conducted national consumer insight research related to car purchases, personal image, depression, obesity, and menopause.

Dawn co-produced two award-winning educational videos: an instructional video on careers in anthropology (sold through the American Anthropological Society) and a consumer education video on Southwest arts and artists. This video, owned by Northern Arizona University, informs consumers about copycat Native American art and is used in classrooms to teach Navajo students about their heritage.

Dawn is the co-founder of a national youth volunteer organization, **Kids Korps USA**, **kidskorps@triad.rr.com**. The organization engages young people, ages 5-18, in charitable activities and community-based service. Its mission is to instill in America's youth the spirit of giving while providing valuable education in leadership and responsibility. The eight-year-old organization plans to expand nationwide in 2004. In 1999, Dawn and her sister, Joani Wafer (co-founder of Kids Korps) were among nine women awarded *Redbook* magazine's Mothers and Shakers Award for "significant contributions toward promoting peace in America to ensure a safe future for our families and those we love." Her professional and community service work has been cited in more than 100 newspapers and magazines nationwide, and she continues to give talks on numerous topics at conferences, workshops, schools, and civic organization meetings. Currently, Dawn is teaming up with Joani Wafer and Joanne Wolf, Ph.D., to write a series of books about youth volunteerism.

Dawn is married to Charlie Lehman; has two children, Steve and Kyle Romund; two stepchildren, Scott and Matt Lehman; and three grandchildren, Robert Gibson and Michael and

Matthew Romund. Her dog, Meistro, continues to remind her to chill out when things get stressful. She was born on December 20, 1948, in Syracuse, New York. She grew up and raised her children in the suburbs of Detroit. She is the oldest of eight children – four girls and four boys. Her loving brother, who is four years her junior, thinks he is the oldest.

"The key for all of us
who want to make a difference is to act.
To do something, anything.
That's the key that will unlock the door
to a future unimagined by so many people.
Sometimes...we feel powerless,
unable to do anything.
Just one act,
anything you can think of,
can restart your engine."
-- W. Mitchell

Irene Levitt

Do you generally feel respected as a woman?
Yes, very much so.

What is your own personal definition of "respect"?
Showing deference or regard to and by others.

What did you do differently than most women to get where you are?
I understood what to expect from people through my study of handwriting analysis. I have three degrees in handwriting analysis and it has been a significant tool in my life in two ways (1) to understand myself and (2) to understand others.

Was respect something you had to consciously work to achieve?
My business is more difficult than most because some people still think of it as some kind of voodoo. I have to be really good at what I do because there are no second chances. In addition, I believe that I have been respected as a handwriting expert because I immediately set myself up as a business-person with an office address, business phone number, and an ad in the yellow pages, etc.

I treat men the same way I treat women except I often make it a point to discuss sports. I'm a fan of baseball, basketball and tennis. I'm aware of the names of major players and make it a point to read the sport pages daily. That has proven to be an asset, but only with men.

Are the factors that create respect at work the same factors as those that create respect at home?

Absolutely. I expect directness and honesty and I receive what I give. I strive to be an objective thinker (keep the emotions for love relationships, please) and this works wonders, especially in the business world.

What would you advise women to do to be taken seriously – by men and women?
Dressing appropriately for your profession is extremely important. Traditionally, "feminine," i.e. high heels, see-through blouses, mini-skirts, etc. might get you a boy friend, but will not earn you respect in the business world.

Be yourself and cross your **T's** at least three quarters of the way **up** the stem, with a long and strong crossing! That indicates a higher feeling of self-worth and purpose. You'll be ready to tackle anything!

Irene Levitt: 1985-2003,President of Handwriting Consultants, LLC, which provides forensic analysis; document examination; criminal investigation; jury screening; self-awareness training and compatibility of management and love relationships.

1985, Master's Degree in Graphoanalysis. College Instructor in handwriting analysis from 1985 until the present.

1979-1990, Casting Director for Major Motion Pictures & Television such as the award-winning 10-hour mini-series, "Lonesome Dove." Worked with Sean Connery, Bette Midler, Robert Duvall, etc.

Author of three books on handwriting analysis. The latest, *"Brainwriting! Enrich Your Life Using Handwriting Analysis"* is available worldwide and at www.**irenelevitt.com.**

Additional Skills: Professional pianist and pilot.

Married for eight years to Sheldon Sigesmund. Our first spouses are deceased and together we have five children and eight grandchildren. No pets this year.

I was born on March third, in Pittsburgh, Pennsylvania and was raised there. I have two older brothers and one younger sister. I was kind of in the middle, but the oldest daughter. My sister and I were born on the same day, two years apart. Her daughter and my son were born on the same day, same year.

"Courage manifests only in the presence of fear.
Taking a step in a new direction,
where we've never been before,
can be uncomfortable, sometimes frightening.
Our other option
is to stand still and never move at all."
--- Mary Manin Morrissey

Linda Lindsey

Do you generally feel respected as a woman?
Yes.

What is your own personal definition of "respect"?
Treating people with personal dignity, taking time to listen and to acknowledge and, as much as possible, accepting differences.

What did you do differently than most women to get where you are?
I extract meaning from all experiences. I asked myself, "What is the most important thing to do in this situation?" I presented myself in a professional manner in a professional setting and I took advantage of learning opportunities.

Was respect something you had to consciously work to achieve?
Only in the earliest days of my career. I often asked myself, "Who is the best person and the best professional I can be in this situation?" I tried to live up to that image.

Are the factors that create respect at work the same factors as those that create respect at home? Yes, with some modifications. Power, control, freedom and fun are common issues in both settings. Pay attention to them all.

What would you advise women to do to be taken seriously – by men and women?
♀   A professional is one who does what needs to be done, when it needs to be done, whether or not she feels like it.
♀   Make your work your passion.

♀ Do a good job on the 'filler' as well as on the major pieces of your work."

Women need to develop a network of power. If you can't pull another woman up the ladder after you, at least point out where the ladder is.

Linda Lindsey
-President of Lindsey Consulting Group, Inc.

-Conducts instructional design and delivery training in a brain-based model and leadership development training for public and private sector organizations in this country and abroad.

-Served as Project Director for a one-year project that analyzed three funds coming to a California company; planned and facilitated more than 70 community meetings to discuss, identify and prioritize compelling needs; and prepared recommendations for investing $200+million over a period of 20 years to improve the quality of life.

-Working with business partner, facilitated 25 community focus groups meetings in seven counties in North Carolina to identify community assets that serve children ages 0 - 5 and their families and to solicit prioritized suggestions for strengthening current assets and creating new ones; prepared 287-page database report to be used as a planning tool in the seven-county area.

-Established and directed the management training division of an executive educational consultant company.

-Directed North Carolina's five training schools for adjudicated juvenile delinquents. Supervised 700+ staff and managed $26 million budget. During time of service, training schools earned accreditation by the American Correctional Association.

-Conducted instructor development training and management training for companies re-locating to North Carolina from other states and other countries.

-Provided state-level administration for a state-funded employment and training program for the North Carolina Community College System. Program was the only tax-supported education program that received continuation funding on the basis of an earn-back index that reflected the amount of time required for graduates to return to the state, in the form of income increase and welfare decrease, the amount invested in their training.

-Certified Presenter of The 4MAT System.

-Certified Reality Therapist.

-Former President of the North Carolina Adult Education Association.

-Former President of the North Carolina Women's Political Caucus.

-Ed.D. from North Carolina State University

I am married and have two grown stepchildren and three grandchildren. Birth date: 4/10/49. I am the older of two sisters.

"Follow your instincts.
That's where true wisdom manifests itself."
-- Oprah Winfrey

Pam Lontos

Do you generally feel respected as a woman?
Yes. I was often the only woman on a program or in a position. When you're in sales and making the money, they take you seriously. Clout follows money.

What is your own personal definition of "respect"?
Others asking your advice, getting promoted at work, being included in important meetings, having your opinion sought by others, and being treated nicely.

What did you do differently than most women to get where you are?
I didn't see the barriers. I often say, "Don't tell me it's impossible until after I've already done it!" (which is the title of my book). I just assumed that when I did a good job, I'd get respect. I'd walk in and get the sale and I lived very well on straight commission for 15 years. I always assumed that I'd get it. I'm oblivious to whether or not there is a glass ceiling. Many women are too worried about barriers instead of focusing on what is important to the company's bottom line.

Was respect something you had to consciously work to achieve?
No.

Are the factors that create respect at work the same factors as those that create respect at home?
No. You have to be more careful of feelings at home. When you sell, you speak directly and make statements. At home you must make requests.

**What would you advise women to do to be taken seriously –
by men and women?**

♀ Be important to the bottom line

♀ Take credit for your own contributions

♀ Don't be demanding until you are valuable to the company and they don't want to lose you.

♀ Don't be paranoid when you lose. Ask yourself, "What do I need to do next time to get the job?"

♀ Observe what successful people are doing and do that.

Quit worrying about being a woman and just do the job. Take charge!

Pam Lontos is founder and president of PR/PR, in Orlando, FL, a public relations firm that specializes in getting publicity for speakers and authors. She is the author of *Don't Tell Me It's Impossible Until After I've Already Done It,* published by William Morrow and Co. Pam is a former professional speaker and past Vice President of Sales for Disney's Shamrock Broadcasting. She knows what it takes to successfully promote your speaking career or publicize your book.

Pam has a Masters Degree in Psychology and Advertising from Southern Methodist University, and has sold retail, cars, health club, and media advertising.

She has appeared on the *Phil Donahue Show, PM Magazine, Hour Magazine, Sally Jessy Rafael Show, CBS Live at Five,* and *CNN News.* She has co-hosted her own TV show, *"Whole New You"* on Lifetime Network. She has appeared in

a cover story *of Entrepreneur magazine, Reader's Digest, Esquire, Cosmopolitan* and many other publications. She has been named as one of the six best sales trainers in the country by *Selling Power* magazine.

She is a long-time member of the *National Speakers Association.*

Married to Rick Dudnick (partner in PR firm, too), Kids: Anna Marie (22) lives in Dallas, Ryan (29) in the Navy in Maryland. Pet: Chakra (Chihuahua), Sloopy (sugar glider) Born: February 28, Wichita, KS and raised in Dallas, TX, one younger brother.

Most success springs
from an obstacle or failure.
I became a cartoonist
largely because I failed in my goal
of becoming a
successful executive.
- Scott Adams, of "Dilbert" fame

Petrena Lowthian

Do you generally feel respected as a woman?
Yes, I always have done. I was brought up as a **person** first and always earned the same as a gentleman did.

What is your definition of "respect"?
It's something I never looked for -- I just expect it. Never think of it.

What did you do differently than most women to get where you are?
I found a way to work for myself. I decided I wanted to teach. I started a school with no definite thought. I just did it. Each day, I figured out what was needed to be done. Do what is there in front of you waiting to be done. My motto is, "Bash On Regardless!"

Was respect something you had to consciously work to achieve?
I never thought about it. I think more about what I am doing and less about what **they** are doing.

Are the factors that create respect at work the same as those that create respect at home?
I never considered it. It was never an issue.

What would you advise women to do to be taken seriously – by men and women?
Act and react to your own instincts. Work from your heart; your head makes it so complicated. Do what you want to do, don't spend an extraordinary amount of time planning and don't look for complicated answers. Just do it.

Generally, when people say yes, they mean no. When they say no, they mean yes. If you have a good idea and when people say it isn't good, do it anyway. When you have an idea that they say is good, watch out!

In precise British tones: Be yourself. Do what you want to

do. I know this isn't, "nice," but remember that everyone goes to the bathroom and it's a waste of time being afraid of people. Thinking about others people's opinion of you can waste half of your life.

Petrena Lowthian
Personal: Born in London England, I was the older of two girls, sister Janice. Married, 2 grown sons.

Education: Scotland High School, Royal Academy Of Arts, London, Clayton Merchandising, London
Career: modeling, retailing, theater.
Wolfit Shakespeare Company, with shows in London and all over England
Walter Thompson USA, Kraft Theater
Established Lowthian College, president for 35 years, clothes design, merchandising, interior design.
Member of Downtown Council, Chairperson, Retail Division
Chairperson Council Private Business and Correspondence School of Minnesota
Member and Board Industrial Advisers, University Wisconsin, Stout . Rotary Nine Chair Educational Committee and member, 15 years. Chairperson Fashion Group, Annual Student Fair

Result: A fabulous interesting life.

Marcele L. Martin

Do you generally feel respected as a woman?
Yes.

What is your own personal definition of "respect"?
When your opinion counts, when what you think matters, when your ideas are implemented.

What did you do differently than most women to get where you are?
Not so different. I chose to do what I really loved and that made it easy to become an overachiever. When you love what you do, it's not really work. You just do it. I've also had good strong male support on my path.

Was respect something you had to consciously work to achieve?
I didn't think about it. I just didn't. I learned to assert myself in a way that did not insult others.

Are the factors that create respect at work the same factors as those that create respect at home?
I've been married for 32 years to a man who is comfortable with himself so it is not an issue at home.

At work or in business, the factors are different for many women. At work you can sometimes choose your relationships. The emotional ties are different so the dynamics differ.

What would you advise women to do to be taken seriously – by men and women?
♀   Believe in your self

♀ Forget the "assigned" roles.
♀ When you are self-assured, others will take you seriously.

Think for yourself and believe in yourself and remember that you can move mountains!

Marcele L. Martin: Born in Marche en Famenne, Belgium on October 1, 1947. Immigrated to Canada in 1951. Aside from 2 years in Belgium (1960-1961), education was in Quebec in a parochial school. Then in Florida, and now I am pursuing additional credentials through Mars Hill College.

Graduated High School in 1964 at the age of 16.
Began broadcasting career almost immediately. Worked at the local station for about 2 years, moved onto television.
By the age of 19, was working for the top television station in Quebec City. Started Martin and Associates in 1977, an accounting firm. Also started Career Paths, Inc, a company that focused on seminars for small business and then went on to doing Payroll for Extras in the television and movie industry.
Opened a pub called Mike's Draft House, sold it to move to NC. In 1994, I began broadcasting work again as news director for local radio stations, as well as teaching for the local Community College and working for a CPA firm. In 2000, started a small business and development consulting practice.

I am now developing seminars for both small business and women in business. I have found that women are mostly forgotten when it comes to assistance and recognition. My focus will be on "Women in Transition" women who have come to

a crossroad, and now must face issues that they are not well prepared for.

I will be doing business in both Quebec and the US in the near future. I am in negotiation with businesses in Canada to present seminars and do training in business software. This will happen within the next few months.

I have been married to Mike since 1970. We have a son who is living now in NC and married. We have a granddaughter named Emily and a new one on the way. I am enjoying the new role of grandmother.

I have a dog, a mutt named Oreo. She is a cross between a terrier and a border collie. She came from the shelter. I wanted a small Maltese.... so, in his infinite wisdom, my husband said that Oreo was an Appalachian Maltese. She may not be exactly what I asked for, but she loves me just as much....and she keeps me motivated to walk my mile every morning and every night.

I am presently on the board of Asheville-Buncombe Visions, Neighborhood Housing Service, and the Buncombe County Women Commission, Past board member of the Asheville Buncombe League of Women Voters, the Franklin Rotary International, a charter member of The Franklin Toastmasters Club.

I actively participate in the local chamber of commerce; I am the regional Vice president of the French American chamber of commerce of North Carolina, volunteer with the local Aids programs and I teach continuing education at Asheville Buncombe Community College.

Linda McCabe

Do you generally feel respected as a woman?
I feel respected as a person. It depends a lot upon where I am. In my current environment and in business I do feel respected. When I owned a scrap metal company, I felt respected. Socially, I feel that women are often merely tolerated and that men feel threatened by serious women.

What is your own personal definition of "respect"?
Treat others in a way that makes them feel good and accepted, not wrong.

What did you do differently than most women to get where you are?
I pushed myself beyond comfort. I'm willing to do whatever has to be done in order to be successful. I am resourceful and I find people who can give me answers if I can't find them myself. I refuse to be a victim. I focus on my goal and I move ahead.

Was respect something you had to consciously work to achieve?
Yes. Without achievement I didn't feel worthy of respect. My value is my achievement. Everyone deserves respect, but achievement assures you that you get it.

Are the factors that create respect at work the same factors as those that create respect at home?
No. At home we have to be Martha Stewart first. (Laughing.) At work you are judged by achievement and dollars earned. Ideally, if we're good people, respect will follow.

What would you advise women to do to be taken seriously – by men and women?

♀ Look at the big picture: Be less petty, focus on goals, less on personalities and small stuff.

♀ Appreciate the differences in people and don't spend time judging them,

♀ Make others aware of your talents and don't wait ever-so-patiently for others to recognize them.

♀ Find a mentor or guide.

♀ Don't compare yourself to others. You and your talents are unique.

♀ Be business-like. Follow proven business practices and have a business plan.

WOW!

Words of Wisdom

Trust yourself and keep going!

Linda McCabe: Married, two grown children (boy and girl) and dogs from time-to-time that my daughter boards at our home. Born in Chicago; 11-25-42, grew up on the Westside of Chicago, then in Rogers Park in Chicago, Illinois.

After graduating from the University of Illinois, Urbana, Linda started her career at for Cahners Publishing. Although she had a good opportunity for advancement, she turned to teaching in the Chicago Public Schools in the inner city. She first taught kindergarten, went on to teach second through seventh grades, and served for a while as a Reading Specialist.

Linda raised her two children along with Scooby, their dog, and after teaching for fifteen years, she made a bold move to become a sales rep in her father's scrap iron and metal company. Linda faired very well in a male-dominated industry, and increased her company's customer base ten fold. She became President and ran her company for thirteen years. Having grown the business to over six million in sales, following a dream, she successfully sold her company.

Now she has founded and is President of Feminine Forum. **www.FeminineForum.com,** an advisory board for women, that provides answers and support for professional women.

Linda Chairs the Corporate Development Committee of the National Association of Women Business Owners, Chicago Chapter, sits on the Advisory Board of the U.S. Women's Chamber of Commerce, and is V.P. of Education for her Toastmaster's Plus Club.

Linda is an avid exerciser as a runner and a walker, and takes step class, does strength training at home, and machine work at her health club. Other interests include reading movies, and promoting success for women.

Love is a force more formidable than any other.
It is invisible – it cannot be seen or measured,
yet it is powerful enough
To transform you in a moment,
and offer you more joy
than any material possession could.
- Barbara De Angelis

Cynthia McKay

Do you generally feel respected as a woman?
Yes, I do now. Early on – no, but I set myself on a pathway to demand respect. Women have been led to need affirmation. When I stopped being a lawyer and opened a company to produce gift baskets in 1992 everyone thought I was crazy. Because of this abrupt career change, my respect level in society dropped dramatically and many thought so had my IQ. (Laughing!) I had to work diligently to regain any respect that I could.

What is your definition of "respect"?
I think of respect as having great pride in what I do and I assume that of others as well because respect is a reciprocal endeavor. I also make sure to clarify issues, and I usually set the record straight to establish and maintain reasonable relationships, When communicating with others, I make sure to clarify issues. I set the record straight early on so people understand I'm easy to deal with as well as a no nonsense communicator. This helps to establish and maintain reasonable relationships.

What did you do differently than most women to get where you are?
I appreciated my androgynous qualities. I impulsively quit being a lawyer and decided to make this change on my own without opting to get the opinions of others. I decided for once in my life to be completely true to myself. I sketched out a close to perfect lifestyle and walked into this change, feeling very secure about my decision.

Was respect something you had to consciously work to achieve?
(Laughing) I think so with the career change. *A lawyer to gift baskets?* They said, "Are you nuts?"

Are the factors that create respect at work the same as those that create respect at home?
My relationship at home is different than work. It is giving and I am much more tolerant at home. Work requires perfection; home is a work of art. Work requires the managing of tasks and personalities among other problems.

There is no *management* per se' at home, I just love to be there. Business relationships emphasize customer service and I am always aware of the power balance as it pertains to work. I want no power issues at home.

What would you advise women to do to be taken seriously – by men and women?
♀ Live your dreams
♀ Don't look for affirmations or approval from others, just do it!
♀ Do your homework, research and follow through.
♀ Stay focused
♀ Surround yourself with positive people.

Utilize all the tools that you can gather and follow your own path. Whether you're at home, work or getting an education, it's not easy no matter what you choose to do…because, as we say in the south, "If Mama ain't happy, nobody's happy!"

WOW!

Words of Wisdom

Cynthia McKay:
Studied art and political science at the University of London.
BA in communications from the University of Central Florida,
Juris Doctorate (law) University of Denver.

Currently CEO of Le Gourmet Gift Basket, Inc. a franchising
corporation. I currently advise and oversee 510 worldwide
franchises.

As an attorney I was dismayed by the profession of law. One
day I abruptly quit my job, opened a home-based gift basket
business and grew into the franchising operation. Known as
an expert in home businesses, I have appeared on numerous
television shows including *CNN, Lifetime, Discovery Channel, Ananada Lewis*. Also I have been a subject of various articles including media such as: Washington Post, Wall Street
Journal, NY Times, Cover of Woman's World Magazine, First
for Women, and more.

In addition to my CEO position, I am currently a law professor in the evenings at a local University. I have just started a
foundation to assist injured animals in need of medical care.

I am a former backup singer for Tiny Tim. It was at that point
in my show business career that I knew I needed regimentation and discipline.

FAMILY: Married 10 years to Paul Gomez. We met in law
school and he is the Assistant Attorney General of Colorado.
No children but a fabulous dog, Keeana (she's a Samoyed).
Born January 31, 1955 up north (much to my father's chagrin-
he was a southerner) but immediately moved to Orlando
Florida so I could be raised south of the Mason-Dixon line. I
am the baby to two much older brothers. My father was 55
when I was born, my mother 45.

Joni Metolius, MS, MFT

Do you generally feel respected as a woman?
Yes.

What is your own personal definition of "respect"?
To be respectful of others, I consider their feelings, the situation, the greater implications and I try to provide clean, clear and gracious communication.

What did you do differently than most women to get where you are?
I felt no limitations in what I could do and become in the world. I was encouraged to feel that I could do what I wanted to do. I rarely felt discriminated against as a woman. Perhaps that was because I grew up around creative and talented people. (Laughing!)

I always believed that I was capable of doing something to make a difference and that I had the stamina to do so.

Was respect something you had to consciously work to achieve?
Yes. I recall in third grade not feeling respected by my peers, and that baffled me. Later on in life I found it was important for me to clearly understand the expectations of others in order to feel respected. For example, what was expected of me in the work environment.

Relationships in general have some simple guidelines for respect such as being impeccable with my word. Also, as I grew up, I wanted to feel respected by my father but I felt I

had been a disappointment to him. That drove me to set goals and to follow them to earn his respect.

Are the factors that create respect at work the same factors as those that create respect at home?
Yes, as I mentioned, what I do in the work environment and what I do in relationships to achieve respect are the same.

What would you advise women to do to be taken seriously – by men and women?
Respect starts with each of us respecting ourselves and works outward from there. Here are some wonderful codes of ethics for personal behavior out there that serve me.

♀ From Shakespeare's Hamlet, "To thine own self be true."
♀ The first agreement from *The Four Agreements*, "Be impeccable with your word."
♀ A Buddhist principal, "Do no harm."

To be respected,
one must act respectfully.
Respect yourself and you'll
function respectfully to others.

Joni Metolius
The love of my life is in England. I have no kids, live with my domestic companion, a Golden Retriever, Bubba John. On 5/18/42, I was born in Portland, Oregon, grew up with an older brother in an area outside of Portland.

Private Practice, Novato, CA June 1977-Present
Implementing problem resolutions with individuals and groups in areas of substance abuse recovery issues; treating

trauma survivors; instituting programs improving personal performance in career and relationships; devising programs reducing chronic pain, critical incident de-briefings.

Thrivesite™ Founder, Development Director Novato, CA February 1996-Present Developing on-line educational/ motivational software product for HMO's and EAP's

Consultant, trainer, lecturer, and author, Novato, CA June 1977-Present Writing articles, developing and presenting programs for television, radio, individuals, industry, and treatment facilities, regarding long and short term psychological effects of physical, sexual traumas, and natural disasters, stress management, conflict resolution.

State of California, Board of Registered Nursing, July 1990-Present
Diversion Evaluation Committee
Bank of America Drug and Alcohol Program, San Francisco, CA 1988-1989
Time Out, San Rafael, CA April 1987- December 2000

EDUCATION AND TRAINING:
California State University - Hayward, CA Master's, Clinical Counseling, Industrial Setting Internship – Chevron International, Employee Assistance Program
University of California/Berkeley - Haas School of Business Entrepreneurial Fast Track
Portland State University - Portland, OR Bachelor's, Political Science
State of California - Standard Teaching Credential, State of California - Hypnosis Certification.

Terri Ouellette

Do you generally feel respected as a woman?
Yes, as I have become more successful I have felt more respected. People listen to me now. I am also more mature and by virtue of what I do, they have to listen to what I say. (Laughing!) And when people don't listen to me or respect me – I move on.

What is your own personal definition of "respect"?
Listening carefully is a big aspect of respect to me. And the listening is not only being listened to and listening to others, it's also is essential that you listen to *yourself*. Are you listening to your head or to your heart? I also feel respected when people ask my advice and carefully considered using it. Listening is huge.

What did you do differently than most women to get where you are?
I am very fortunate to have a great family, a wonderful support system and my husband is my biggest fan. In TV, for a long time, I had to work for free to gain experience and credentials. Many times things would go wrong and my mantra became, "There has to be a reason." I've always kept my eyes and ears open for opportunities and when they presented themselves I just went for it.

Was respect something you had to consciously work to achieve?
No, not at all. I've always tried to do my best and to do things that made me happy. I always do good work, I'm always dependable and I hate to disappoint others and the logical by-product has been respect.

Are the factors that create respect at work the same factors as those that create respect at home?
In a sense, yes. Consistency, keeping your word and follow through are as important at home as they are work. The trust issues are all the same,

What would you advise women to do to be taken seriously – by men and women?
♀ Consistently be YOU. Don't put up a façade.
♀ Figure out who you are and what you want to accomplish, create a vision and a plan, and then JUST DO IT. Spend less time thinking and more time doing.

Everyone deserves everything! Think of yourself as a powerful, smart, creative person. Think less about being a woman and more about being a person.

Terri Ouellette
This Emmy Award-winning television personality has been the reigning "Craft Queen" of the Southwest for the past 9 years. **www.terriocreations.com**. Terri O uses her high energy and passion for creating to inspire even the most "craft challenged." Her unconventional "how-to" approach has created quite a following. She's fun, witty and makes her fair share of mistakes. Every level of crafter learns something-- even if it's what not to do.

Terri O says, "If I can't use it, why do it? Hey I'm a Mom and have a career. I don't have time to mess around!"

Terri Ouellette has worked in television for 13 years as a news anchor, show host and special features reporter. *"Home with Terri O"* debuted in 1999 and has remained the number one show on Saturday mornings in Arizona. That show also earned her an Emmy in June of 2001. Terri O also features some of her favorite products for creating on QVC. Terri O tours the U.S. as the National Spokesperson for the *Hobby Industry Association.*

Terri O lives in Arizona with her husband and two young sons Kyle 11 and Tatum 6. She has the largest assortment of glue guns you have ever seen!

Nothing of importance is ever
achieved without discipline.
I feel myself sometimes not wholly
in sympathy with some modern
educational theorists,
because I think that they underestimate
the part that discipline plays.
But the discipline you have in your life
should be one determined
by your own desires and your own needs,
not put upon you by society or authority.
- Bertrand Russell

Constance Porteous

Do you generally feel respected as a woman?
Yes, but I don't feel that early childhood education, as a profession, is respected.

What is your own personal definition of "respect"?
Respect is a feeling that is generated when someone listens and gives credence to what you say. In addition, I think that respect is based on trust. Trust that you will be listened to, as well that you will listen to the other person.

What did you do differently than most women to get where you are?
I don't know if I did anything differently. I took risks; I did things spontaneously. I think my sense of history helped. Wherever I went, I felt like I was touching some part of history. I went off to Europe and took chances. I came home and followed a dream to not only teach but to marry and be a mother. Strange combination. (Laughing!)

Was respect something you had to consciously work to achieve?
Yes. First I had to learn respect for myself. Once that was accomplished then I felt that others listened to me more. That process took a long time.

Are the factors that create respect at work the same factors as those that create respect at home?
I think so. The way you carry yourself, the way you feel about yourself, all of that is projected outward and you get it back. The more quality there is in a relationship, the easier it is to experience mutual respect, but it is not as easy as that. It

takes a lot of work and it takes a lot of reflection. Believing in yourself will only take you so far. (Laughing!) Others have their baggage and may not be able to meet you halfway.

What would you advise women to do to be taken seriously – by men and women?

♀ Believe in yourself.

♀ Don't pretend to be something you're not - you are a woman, not a man.

♀ What you believe in, what you do, what you accomplish, has to be the important part, not the gender.

Katharine Hepburn, Eleanor Roosevelt, Marian Wright Edelman, and Cokie Roberts are all wonderful examples of women who say, "This is who I am. Take me or leave me."

I have many women whom I admire; not all are the most famous. Some are women who just decided to take the same path, to search for themselves and accept themselves. It takes a lifetime.

Constance Porteous, Early Childhood Educator.
I was born in New York City. I grew up on the West side of Manhattan. I spent wonderful years in New York. I loved exploring that city. I don't miss it, except occasionally. Born: 5-18-40. I have a brother, two years older. Family: Husband, 3 children, 4 cats, 2 dogs over time.

Education:
Elementary School- City and Country, New York City (Private)

Ethical Culture Schools (Private)
High School- Ethical Culture Schools (Private)
College - Oberlin College, Oberlin, Ohio
Graduate School - Columbia University, Teachers College, New York City.
Post Graduate Courses: Oakton Community College, National Louis University

I am responsible.
Although I may not be able
to prevent the worst from happening,
I am responsible for my attitude
toward the inevitable misfortunes
that darken life.
Bad things do happen;
how I respond to them defines my character
and the quality of my life.
I can choose to sit in perpetual sadness,
immobilized by the gravity of my loss,
or I can choose to rise from the pain
and treasure the most precious gift I have
...life itself.
Walter Anderson

Valerie A. Rawls

Do you generally feel respected as a woman?
Yes. I conduct myself in a manner that shows that I respect and honor others, and it is reflected back. *Dirty mirrors have to go!*

What is your own personal definition of "respect"?
You demonstrate respect when you show consideration for the opinions, thoughts and ideas of others. When you hold others in high esteem, it often comes back. You are worthy of respect when you live a moral life and are attuned and concerned with the global perspective.

What did you do differently than most women to get where you are?
I listened to a strong man! I was never caught up in that "boy-girl" thing. I've listened to wise men and wise women. My father taught me a lot and gave me a leg up. I've always been confident in my own thoughts and actions and comfortable with who I am.

Was respect something you had to consciously work to achieve?
No. I had loving parents who instilled a high level of self-esteem in me, but they also taught me that respect is earned and not given. When I was young, I had to harness my self-confidence because sometimes it threatened others. I get a lot of respect and I give it as well.

Are the factors that create respect at work the same factors as those that create respect at home?

I like to think so. My husband and I try to exude the same behavior at home and at work. Why would I treat my co-workers any better than my children? We value the opinions of others, and demonstrate it at all times.

What would you advise women to do to be taken seriously – by men and women?
Value your own opinions, as well as the opinions of others. It is obvious when you respect the ideals and values of others. Hopefully people will base their opinion of you on who you are and not just what you do.

Other women are not the enemy. We don't have to jockey for position; we should nurture each other! Create your own Old Girl Network.

We need more Ruth and Naomi relationships. We need to learn how to have relationships in which we can give and receive support. Agree to disagree, and still embrace each other.

Valerie Rawls, President and Founder of *Hill Rawls Design Ink*: Her experience ranges from graphic design, production coordination and art direction of major publications such as, Ebony and Jet in addition to other corporate marketing communication experience. It is through these experiences and accomplishments that led her to develop *Hill Rawls Design Ink*.

Mrs. Rawls is the founding principal and president of the award winning marketing firm, Hill Rawls Design Ink, **www.hrdi.net**, located in Schaumburg, IL. Her clients have

ranged from start up companies to global organizations including telecommunication giants like Ameritech, ATT and Covad, financial services clients Computershare, MasterCard, Visa and Wells Fargo. Corporate communications, and industry leading clients include Allstate, Baxter Healthcare, Commonwealth Edison, Quaker Oats and Kraft Food Products to name a few.

Valerie's education and degrees include studies with a design and marketing concentration at Illinois State University, and the American Academy of Art. Mrs. Rawls is a member of the American Marketing Association, a board member of the Schaumburg Business Association and Horizons for Youth. She contributes freely to select non-profit organizations and was featured in the March 2002 issue of *Essence Magazine*.

Valerie and Elbert have been married for eighteen years. They are the parents of two wonderful children Erica and Evan. Her birthday 8-1-58, she was born and raised in Elkhart, IN. She is the oldest of three girls.

The greatest discovery you'll ever make
is the potential of your own mind.
- Jose Silva

Cokie Roberts

Do you generally feel respected as a woman?
Yes I do, now that I'm an older woman! (Laughing!) They don't take you seriously until you're 50! For many years I felt like I was invisible to both men and women. People would talk to my husband and ignore me. One night, at a party, a man said, "What do you do?" When I mentioned that I produced a TV show, I instantly became the center of attention. I find it horrendous that you only get respect when you do something "important" or highly visible or have a fancy title.

Any woman who's raised children knows how very hard it is. But after one gets the little darlings to bed, one can read interesting books. So mothers at home are often far better read than those on the corporate treadmill.

What is your own personal definition of "respect"?
I subscribe to the Golden Rule and treat others as I wish to be treated. One of the things that truly upsets me is watching couples in public, especially with children in public, and listening to how couples talk to each other and how they talk to their children. It is often the least respectful communication you'll ever hear.

What did you do differently than most women to get where you are?
I don't think I did anything differently. I was perhaps in the right time and place. What I did differently was to maintain balance and it was a struggle.

Women older than I am did marriage, children and work in the community. Those were our expectations too, and we got

as far as the getting married and having children young, but then we all went to work.

My family always came first because that's where my priorities are. It helped that the children did come chronologically before the professional climb, so that meant there was no question about priorities.

Was respect something you had to consciously work to achieve?
Absolutely. Particularly when I first joined THIS WEEK with David Brinkley. It was a very fine line you had to walk. You couldn't be a wallflower but you could not be as aggressive as a man. Not too quiet, but not too imposing or else they would call you that word that rhymes with witch. You had to be very respectful but assertive enough so that there was a point to your being there. I knew I had to earn the respect of my viewers and colleagues - especially my colleagues. I knew that if I worked hard and knew my stuff, I would get their respect. That was not an era where an "in your face" attitude would work. (Laughing!)

Are the factors that create respect at work the same factors as those that create respect at home?
To the degree that you create respect by being respectful, yes. In the work that I do there's a certain amount of performance involved and *that* is different than it is at home. In fact, performing at home is not looked upon kindly...by anybody. (Laughing!)

What would you advise women to do to be taken seriously – by men and women?
♀ Dress seriously. You can't wear bare midriffs to work and expect to be taken seriously.

♀ Know your stuff. We've always had to work harder and know more than men to get taken seriously.

♀ Do your homework. Be prepared for all eventualities, armed with knowledge, statistics and resources.

Listen to your mother! She's generally right because she's lived longer and has a wealth of accumulated wisdom.

COKIE ROBERTS
ABC News Chief Congressional Analyst

Cokie Roberts is the chief congressional analyst and a political commentator for ABC News. She covers politics, Congress and public policy for ABC News, reporting for "World News Tonight" and other ABC News broadcasts. From 1996 - September 2002 she was the co-anchor of *"This Week with Sam Donaldson and Cokie Roberts."*

In addition to her work for ABC, Ms. Roberts serves as a senior news analyst for National Public Radio, where she was the congressional correspondent for more than ten years. In that time, she won numerous awards, including the highest honor in public radio, the Edward R. Murrow Award. She was also the first broadcast journalist to win the highly prestigious Everett McKinley Dirksen Award for coverage of Congress.

Ms. Roberts is the recipient of numerous other broadcasting awards, including a 1991 Emmy for her contribution to the ABC News special, "Who is Ross Perot?"

Ms. Roberts is the author of the national best seller, "We Are Our Mother's Daughters." The book, published in 1998, explores the diverse roles women have played throughout American history and the connections and distinctions among different generations of women. She is currently at work on a book, "Founding Mothers," which will be published by William Morrow early next year.

Along with her husband, Steven V. Roberts, a professor at George Washington University and contributing editor at U.S. News & World Report, Ms. Roberts writes a weekly column syndicated by United Media in major newspapers around the country. Her Op-Ed columns have appeared in The New York Times and The Washington Post; she has also written for The New York Times Magazine and The Atlantic. In February 2000 they published "From This Day Forward," an account of their more than 30-year marriage, as well as other marriages in American history. It immediately hit the top 10 on the New York Times best-seller list.

Before joining ABC News in 1988, Ms. Roberts was a contributor to PBS-TV's "MacNeil/Lehrer News Hour." Her coverage of the Iran/Contra affair for that program won her the Weintal Award in 1987.

Prior to joining NPR, Ms. Roberts was a reporter for CBS News in Athens, Greece. She also produced and hosted a public affairs program on WRC-TV in Washington, D.C.

From 1981 to 1984, in addition to her work at NPR, she co-hosted "The Lawmakers," a weekly public television program on Congress. Ms. Roberts is former president of the Radio and Television Correspondent's Association.

A 1964 graduate in political science from Wellesley College, Ms. Roberts received a 1985 Distinguished Alumnae Achievement Award in recognition of "excellence and distinction in professional pursuits." She is the recipient of 15 honorary degrees. Ms. Roberts and her husband are the parents of two adult children.

Aim for success, not perfection.
Never give up your right to be wrong,
because then you will lose the ability
to learn new things
and move forward with your life.
Remember that fear always lurks
behind perfectionism.
Confronting your fears and allowing
yourself the right to be human
can, paradoxically,
make yourself a happier
and more productive person.
- Dr. David M. Burns

Letitia Lovely Robinson

Do you generally feel respected as a woman?
Yes, I feel respected in a number of roles -- as a leader, mother, wife, daughter, sister and friend. On a professional level and personal level, I strive to add value where I can and I believe my contributions are respected.

What is your own personal definition of "respect"?
A high regard and value for individuals that is demonstrated and acted upon. Acceptance is at the very core of respect for one's self and others. Making a conscious choice to accept people for who they are demonstrates a willingness to respect and be respected. Respect is a vital component for interacting with others.

What did you do differently than most women to get where you are?
Placed my trust in God, not man. I learned from my experiences. I sought wisdom from those I respect by listening, observing and assessing their impact on the lives of others. Most of all, I have learned to honor and respect balance -- work hard, play hard, and pray hard! (Laughing!)

Was respect something you had to consciously work to achieve?
Yes, and it's an ongoing process. Remember circumstances change behaviors. Once respect is earned, it may never completely erode, but it can certainly change. Be in touch with your environment and be mindful of your expectations. Seek mutual respect and be ready to receive what you expect.

Are the factors that create respect at work the same factors as those that create respect at home?

No. At home you have an established environment that is tied together by love. At work it is often a competitive rather than collaborative environment, and they all bring their own baggage (prejudices) to the table.

Honest, open communication is an important factor in both places but it's not always given nor received exactly the same way. The agreements and disagreements are different and the relationships are very different. The inherent factors that create respect at home may be completely foreign to the workplace.

What would you advise women to do to be taken seriously – by men and women?

♀ Understand and validate your role in the workplace and commit to fulfilling your role with a passion.
♀ Stay focused on your purpose, convey confidence and communicate your purpose to others!
♀ Be direct -- give and receive feedback -- make it and take it professionally, not personally!
♀ Learning is a lifelong process -- learn about yourself, your environment and those with whom you interact. Love and respect yourself and others.

Be adaptable and open to giving and growing. To whom much is given, much is expected!

Letitia Robinson: 20 years in corporate America -- 5 years in field sales and 15 years in Training & Development with a Sales focus
Industries I've worked in:
Telecommunications, Office Equipment, Environmental Services, Information Solutions.
Senior Manger of Sales Training, Corporate Learning Center, Experian, Schaumburg, IL (8 years)
ASTD member, CCASTD (former VP of Programming))
Delta Sigma Theta Sorority, Inc. - International Public Service Organization, Member since 1980
Charter Member of Schaumburg-Hoffman Estates Alumnae Chapter BS in Business Administration, Roosevelt University, Chicago, IL

Married to Robbie Robinson, 15 years -- 2 children: 9 year old Lania and 2-year-old Royce.

Born: November 7th, in Starkville, MS left at 6 months and grew up in Chicago, IL. I was the second child born to my parents, Joe & Mary Alice. I have an older brother Kelvin, and a younger sister, Lynette.

Accepting responsibility
is the fulcrum point
for succeeding at anything.
- Jeffrey Gitomer

Patricia A. Scherer, Ph.D.

Do you generally feel respected as a woman?
Yes. I feel respected. Sometimes I do not feel included by my male peers, although they do seem to care.

What is your own personal definition of "respect"?
Respect includes giving you credence for your contribution, you are listened to and your ideas sometimes are put into action and you're not patronized.

What did you do differently than most women to get where you are?
I persevered. I was born into a struggling family during the Depression. There was no support available. I faced tragedy and hard times and learned to ignore that and move forward. I became very self-sufficient.

I learned to delve deeply into things to find answers. If you look long enough and hard enough you will find answers and that is a life skill. Including things on sale! (Laughter!)

Was respect something you had to consciously work to achieve?
Not consciously, but I worked diligently and earned respect as a by-product of that effort. (In spite of much "head-patting" at the University. *Laughing.*) I was always me and respected as me. It was never about **them** — nor would I change for them.

Are the factors that create respect at work the same factors as those that create respect at home?

In many instances. The same positive attributes apply in both places

What would you advise women to do to be taken seriously?

♀ Make the decision that no one can stop you – only you can do that.

♀ Be serious about what you want to accomplish.

♀ Put forth quality efforts and respect is inevitable.

To be a woman is a gift because you're endowed with the same intelligence as men plus you have been given insight into the emotional and spiritual life of those with whom you relate. Insight plus intellect is an unbeatable combination!

Patricia Scherer: I'm married and we celebrated our 50th wedding anniversary last June. We had two girls. My oldest daughter was diagnosed with MS when she was about 31. She passed away 2 ½ years ago leaving 3 daughters, two of whom work at the Center with me. The youngest lives with us and is a college freshman. My youngest daughter lives in Arlington Heights and has 5 children.

My husband took an early retirement from his job with United Technologies as a salesman of telephone switchboard systems to the railroads and public utilities. He then came to the Center and taught himself printing and does all the printing for us.

My hobbies are music, sales-shopping and the arts. All my

grandchildren know me as the person who can find anything you want for the cheapest price possible.

I was born in Chicago Oct. 14th. 1930. I lived here until I was twelve and that was during the Second World War. I was an only child so no interesting position in the family structure. I went to 4 different grade schools, 3 here and 1 in New York and 2 high schools in Florida and Chicago.

I graduated from Amundsen High School at the tender age of 16 and entered Northwestern University as a music major. I moved to Missouri to teach school when I was 20, met my husband, lived there for four years and moved back to Chicago after my husband had a major heart attack when he was 26.

Dr. Patricia Scherer founded the **Center on Deafness** in 1973 as a unique institution dedicated to the provision of equal rights and services to assist in the development of the individual potential of deaf and hard of hearing children, adolescents and adults. It is to this end that each of the programs at the Center was developed. Currently, three corporations are located in the Patricia A. Scherer Building in Northbrook. Mental Health and Deafness is dedicated to the provision of mental health services to those individuals with hearing loss and severe to profound emotional and behavioral disturbances. The Center on Deafness provides mental health services to individuals with hearing loss and moderate to severe emotional and behavioral disorders. The newest corporation is The International Center on Deafness and the Arts (ICODA) dedicated to provide life changing artistic experiences to deaf and hard of hearing children, teens and adults.

ICODA , **www.icoda.com,** and its programs are a realization of Dr Scherer's dreams to provide much-needed cultural experiences to the Deaf community. CenterLight Theatre has pro-

vided both deaf and hearing audiences with quality, professional theater productions in coordinated sign and voice for over twenty years. CenterLight also provides outreach programs for deaf and hearing children and adults which showcase signed theater and the talents of deaf artists. Deaf, hard of hearing and hearing children can also participate in a comprehensive drama program and a dance and signed song troupe, which culminates in a full-scale productions which are open to the public.

Several hundred children have received services at the Center. Many of the children in the Arts Program have gone on to successful professional careers in the Arts, the most successful being, Marlee Matlin, 1987 Academy Award Winner.

Dr. Scherer has a Ph.D. in Psychology of Deafness from Northwestern University in Evanston, Illinois. Her professional experience starts as a grade-school teacher in Missouri and continues as a lecturer in Education of the Hearing Impaired; Assistant Professor, Education of the Hearing Impaired; Director, Teacher Preparation Program; Director, Diagnostic Center for Hearing Impaired Children; Associate Professor, Education of the Hearing Impaired; all at Northwestern University.

Dr. Scherer has been and continues to be a consultant to many state, federal and private institutions including the U.S. Office of Education, Illinois State Board of Education, Illinois Department of Mental Health, Indiana School for the Deaf, Maryland State Department and the Department of Juvenile Research. Because of Dr. Scherer's reputation in the field of deafness, she has been asked to serve on many boards during her career. Currently, Dr. Scherer is the Governor's Appointed Chairman for the Interagency Board for Hearing Impaired/Behavior Disordered Children, the Multi handicapped Committee Chairman for the Conference of Educational Administrators,

Schools for the Deaf and a member of the education committee for the Illinois Deaf Commission.

Dr. Scherer's continued dedication to the deaf culture in the areas of education, mental health and the arts have awarded her many honors. Most recently, Dr. Scherer received the Governor's Certificate of Service Award, U.S. Office of Education Grant for Integrated Theater Programs; Lifetime Achievement Award, Foundation for Hearing and Speech Rehabilitation; and in 1995 was inducted into the North Shore Walk of Fame.

"Everything you want
is out there waiting for you to ask.
Everything you want, wants you.
But you have to take action to get it."
--- Jack Canfield

Rhoberta Shaler, PhD.

Do you generally feel respected as a woman?
Yes, I feel respected as a person.

What is your own personal definition of "respect"?
Treating others in an unbiased way with the expectation of good. I expect the best of others until they prove untrustworthy. I feel respected when people request input, appreciate my work and care what I have to say. Of course, I also feel respected when people treat me well without even knowing who I am…as most healthy people do.

What did you do differently than most women to get where you are?
At ages 17 and 19, I read two important books and understood that I am 100% responsible for what I create in my life. From a redneck, blue-collar background in a small Canadian town, I moved, earned three University degrees as a single Mom with three kids while I was working full-time and receiving no child support. I've walked the hard road and I know well that others can overcome adversity as a result. That's why I now spend my life giving those tools to others to *Optimize Life Now.*

Was respect something you had to consciously work to achieve?
Yes. Yes. I was teaching school in a small town with three kids and I had to learn how to relate better because in a small town everyone knows everything. There are still moments of discrimination to this day, not all are gender specific, and some industries are tougher than others for women.

Are the factors that create respect at work the same factors as those that create respect at home?
Generally yes, except for professional competence, which is required at work.

What would you advise women to do to be taken seriously – by men and women?
♀   Be serious about what you do.
♀   Be passionate!
♀   Accept 100 percent responsibility for teaching others how treat you. Give up victim-hood.
♀   Being respected is a function of presence, self-confidence, and self-esteem.

Have gutsy goals
and take no guff!

International speaker, coach & author, **Rhoberta Shaler, PhD**, is an expert motivator. She works with organizations and individuals who want to shift their results from acceptable to EXCEPTIONAL in life and business. Her enthusiastic approach to life, and success, makes it easy to grasp and apply her practical ideas and insights right away. With her strategies, dreams and plans become measurable achievements.

Through her company, *Optimize Life Now!* ™
www.optimizelifenow.com she offers keynotes and seminars that enhance motivation & self-confidence, improve workplace & client relationships, and build & strengthen their

teams. Each year she gives thousands of people the optimization keys they need to accelerate their desired results.

Dr. Shaler works with direct sales leaders to overcome procrastination, resistance and reluctance to achieving their highest goals.

As an Executive Business Coach, Rhoberta works with individuals and management teams to clarify purpose, promote positive change and transform strategic intentions into measurable results.

B.Ed. - Educational Psychology, M.Ed - Education and Curriculum Development, Ph.D. - Educational Psychology

For eight years, Dr. Shaler owned & operated Serenity Farm Retreat on Vancouver Island in Canada where she offered management retreats and personal development seminars to an international audience.

She has appeared on many radio & television programs including her own series on a Canadian cable network.

Currently, she is the host of the weekly two-hour program, *Optimize Life Now!* ™ on **wsRadio.com**

She has a large online presence through her websites, articles and weekly and bi-weekly ezines. These are available at no charge from her web site, www.OptimizeLifeNow.com

Author of many books & audio programs including *Optimize Your Day: Practical Wisdom for Optimal Living & What You Pay Attention to Expands & Optimize Life Now! The Eight Essentials for Living Richly in Every Way*

Dr. Shaler lives in San Diego, California, where she enjoys the constant sunshine not found in her native Canada.

Jo Smith

Do you generally feel respected as a woman?
Yes.

What is your own personal definition of "respect"?
People listen to what I say and acknowledge my right to my opinion. I feel I am heard.

What did you do differently than most women to get where you are?
I had to succeed. I was 24 with two kids, divorced and we lost *everything* in a flood. I had two kids and nothing else. The Red Cross and Welfare got us a roof over our heads and I had to do something. I researched and found the Top 10 Careers for Women. Sales was one of them and it required no education and provided a good living so I went into sales. Sales and COMMISSIONS were really my only option. Minimum wage wasn't going to get us off of Welfare.

Was respect something you had to consciously work to achieve?
No, I was the first born. I was 2 years old when my 6-month-old brother died of SIDS. I don't remember it at all. But I do know that I became daughter and son that year. I was my Dad's shadow. One of my earliest memories is my Dad telling me 2 things: "You can be anything you want to be" and "You are as good as, not better, than anyone else." He pushed me to be a good student (I was) and I spent more time in the company of adults than children.

Are the factors that create respect at work the same factors as those that create respect at home?

Yes. Personal respect comes from treating others with respect. Communicate! Listen, talk, and agree that we can all get what we want if we talk through conflict. Good negotiating skills are respectful.

What would you advise women to do to be taken seriously – by men and women?

♀ Don't play games.

♀ Learn to share the attention

♀ Learn how to make friends quickly. "Hi, my name is…" And introduce them to others.

♀ Be a survivor, not a victim.

♀ Learn to ask…Ok. Now what?

♀ It's not what you know, it's who you know AND who knows you!

♀ Be a resource and share your knowledge

♀ Starting over is not the end of the world. It is a new beginning.

♀ Don't make others responsible for your happiness.

♀ Don't be needy at work or at home.

Don't burn your bridges. We cross the same rivers many times.

Jo Smith: Creative Connector, Ruiz Agency www.ruizagency.com –full service ad agency/marketing firm and SuperHeroCards.com **www.superherocards.com.** Owner Diogenes Ruiz–a former customer of mine. I sold him his first Macintosh.

Born July 2, 1947 in Lock Haven, Pennsylvania – I'm a Cancer, a Pollyanna and a Survivor. July 2 is the middle day of the year - 182 days before it and after it! The balance point. I was in 13 different schools before I graduated from high school in 1965. We moved again, 3 days after graduation (in Utah).

Married 28 years to my second husband. Three sons: Tom, 35, married to Cora (met in Alaska) 3.5 year old granddaughter, Mia. Peter– 32, Marshall – 24. Peter, Marshall and Richard are all **CHEFS!!!**   2 cats, Knitley and Drake. 1965 – October, my dad died very suddenly of a heart attack at 42.

I'm the OLDEST. One sister –Carol, 5 years younger, two younger brothers.

I've sold computer technology and software for the past 20 years. For 11 years, I was the top sales person for Carolina Computer Stores in Raleigh. My niche was the publishing/advertising market and I sold thousands of Macintosh computers into that market. I won sales contests, prizes, trips, money and most of all –a very loyal client base.

When my husband and I started dating, 28+ years ago, he told me that one of the things that he liked about me was (is) that --- I don't need him. I want him, but I don't need him. He enjoys my strength and is not threatened by it. I also don't try to change him (or anyone else). He said it was refreshing to know that I was not dependent on him for my happiness. We share our days and our life --and I adore him and would be devastated it something happened. And, I would survive.   I think that must come across when I meet other men, too. NO ONE has the power to affect my mood, my day or me unless I allow it.

Marilyn Sprague-Smith
M.Ed. CLL

Do you generally feel respected as a woman?
In my current career as a consultant, author, professional speaker and trainer, absolutely! In my past experiences in corporate America, I did not.

My perception in corporate America was that the glass-ceiling syndrome was real. Lots of dollars were spent on training women for management positions, yet there was little or no evidence of women in the "real" positions on the fast track.

What is your own personal definition of "respect"?
For me, respect is built upon a foundation of trust, and trust is built when we: 1) tell the truth, 2) keep commitments to self and others, and 3) accept personal responsibility for the actions we take and the outcomes that result from our actions.

I believe it's important to act in ways that convey the intent to achieve the highest and best good for all involved. Finally, it's been my experience that we earn respect from others when we choose to value and cherish differences and be non-judgmental.

What did you do differently than most women to get where you are?
Petrena Lowthian, (also interviewed in this book), President of Lowthian College, had a desk plate that said "Bash On Regardless!" I've adopted that as my motto. I just keep moving forward --and scramble when the details reveal themselves. (Laughing.)

I made a conscious choice to be the very best I could be each day. I'm not saying I was perfect, nor that I always acted in ways that were demonstrating "highest and best good for everyone," yet I did what I was capable of doing at the time that I did it. I also learned I needed to learn from my experiences, to be willing to change what needed to be changed and to appreciate the strengths I have and I continue to be willing to embrace the unknown.

I've learned to turn the negatives into life lessons and release judgment, which dissipates my anger. I've learned to forgive, both myself and others. In addition, I learned to lighten up on myself and others so I became a Certified Laughter Leader through the World Laughter Tour. (Laughter.)

Was respect something you had to consciously work to achieve?
Absolutely. First I had to learn to respect myself because I felt that everyone was better than me. I had a huge case of "not good enough." Then I learned that great people see the greatness in others, so I chose to develop a habit of looking for the good in others.

Are the factors that create respect at work the same factors as those that create respect at home?
They are now! My husband and I are an entrepreneurial couple. We co-own a business, as well as share a mutual commitment to our marriage. Because our business is an integral part of our lives, the respect we have for each other's skills and abilities in our business, reinforces the respect we have for each other in our personal lives.

What would you advise women to do to be taken seriously – by men and women?
Choose to honor yourself first. You have to have it within before it can come back from the external. Without self-

respect, you won't recognize respect from others when you get it.

Your authentic self will show up wherever you are and in whatever you are doing. A "good front" will eventually show up. If you don't like who you are right now, choose to do something about it. Be willing to embrace the actions you need to take to become the person you want to be. Then, take the first step and Bash On Regardless!

Marilyn Sprague-Smith, M.Ed., CLL
Married to W. Steele Smith, Jr. CDR. USN (Ret.) aka Commander Rock. Step Children Staci Angel and David Steele Smith, Grandchildren. Brianna Nicole Billiott, -10, Hunter Braedon Angel - 6, Amelia McKenzie Smith- 5,Madeleine Paige Smith – 4 months

I was born June 13, 1951, Fargo, ND. lived in Moorhead, MN until I was in middle school; our family moved to Wahpeton, ND. Two Sisters, Melva Wozniak, Las Vegas, NV and Marlene Schultz, Green Valley, AZ. And me – I'm the youngest of the three!

Graduated from Wahpeton Senior High School, Wahpeton, ND. Graduate of Lowthian College and University of Minnesota; Minneapolis, MN; Lived and built career in Minneapolis, MN over a 25-year timeframe.

Moved to North Carolina in 1991, where I currently live; am a principal of Miracles & Magic, Inc.

www.miraclesmagicinc.com, a consulting business that works with organizations that want to put their mission into action and with leaders who want to breathe new life into their communities.

Marilyn Sprague-Smith, M.Ed., CLL
Aka "Can-Do Princess"
Marilyn Sprague-Smith is a catalyst for long-term, positive change. As a principal and co-founder of Miracles & Magic, Inc., she works with organizations that want to put their mission into action and with leaders who want to breathe new life into their communities. Marilyn is an entrepreneurial, results-oriented consultant, author, professional speaker, trainer and certified laughter leader who consistently designs and delivers programs that harmonize group dynamics, enhance quality of work life and produce bottom line results.

In 2002, Marilyn co-founded The Princess Principle Partners and co-authored *"The Princess Principle: Women Helping Women Discover Their Royal Spirit."* This book, the first in a series focusing on women who want to develop their personal and professional lives, is a message of hope which excels in sunny smiles, aligning hearts and connecting spirit - the Royal Spirit within.

Marilyn earned her Masters Degree in Work, Family and Community Education from the University of Minnesota. She is the 2003 winner of the revered Larry Wilson Award, presented annually to an outstanding educator in a non-school-based setting by the University of Minnesota's College of Education and Human Development Alumni Society. She has earned the prestigious Distinguished Toastmaster Award from Toastmasters International. In addition, she was awarded the 2000-2001 Helen Yandle Award from the NC District of Toastmasters International for outstanding service

as Club President. Her professional memberships include National Speakers Association (NSA), NSA/Carolinas, American Association for Therapeutic Humor and she serves on the Professional Advisory Committee of the World Laughter Tour.

Drawing on her vast range of experiences, from life inside Fortune 500 Companies to First Lady of a North Carolina community, Marilyn weaves masterful stories that inspire her audiences to embrace the future with optimism. Marilyn Sprague-Smith has the gift of touching the hearts of her audience in a way that encourages them to change their behavior and achieve better outcomes.

Ability is what you're capable of.
Motivation determines what you do.
Attitude determines how well you do it.
- Lou Holtz

Lorraine G. Stephens

Do you generally feel respected as a woman?
Let me focus on "generally" and "respected." If we are talking about my professional life, that respect level has changed over the years. Because my field is a technical one, clients often expected a male to arrive to discuss their technical issues.

There was a strong element of surprise when I entered the door. So I knew that my first role was to demonstrate my capabilities before I discussed the specifics of their business. This hurdle is normally not one that a man has to overcome. Fortunately that challenge is not as great today because my name is well recognized and respected in my field. However, as I have the opportunity to work with new clients, I enter the meeting with the full realization that I may have that hurdle before me.

If we are talking about my personal life - yes I do. Because I fully expect the mechanics, and repair men to attempt to take advantage of females, I enter those environments "armed." Before long, they too respect the female customer that they are preparing to serve. Of course my friends and associates just see me as a person. Gender, fortunately, does not have to play a part.

What is your own personal definition of "respect"?
I feel respected when people are able to accept my point of view without the need to change it; "agreeing to disagree" is the phrase we often hear. Respect is also not prejudging - even when our backgrounds are different. When someone takes the time to get to know me before forming an opinion of me - they have demonstrated an element of respect.

What did you do differently than most women to get where you are?
I stepped out. Many people hide in a security blanket. It is unfortunate but they have no foundation for stepping out - nothing to step out *on*. I stepped out on faith - that rules out most people.

The average person wants to be assured of the outcome. Failure was not allowed into the picture - a momentary fall was accepted and understood. There is no doubt in my mind that I can win this race - the only doubt that sometimes crept into my mind was whether or not I could keep running. I keep a piece of writing in front of me that constantly reminds me that the race is already won - I just have to keep running. When I ventured out I did not have any savings to depend on, but I had a strong faith that it could work

While working in the corporate world, I measured success by "levels" and "dollars." Then one day I realized that I was too busy to really enjoy my kids, and they were growing up. At that moment I began to redefine my definition of success. "Levels" meant nothing anymore. Instead spending time with my children, providing for them, being able to educate them and keeping us comfortable as a family, became the core of my definition of success. Based on this definition - I have been successful.

Was respect something you had to consciously work to achieve?
In many cases - yes. I was always a minority - a female math major, the only female in the physics class, the only female manager on the management team, etc. There were times when I found it difficult to fit in with my male counterparts because they already had their network and supported each

other. As a result, I, giving 120% of my efforts, had to demonstrate that I was capable and that I belonged. But I would be remiss if I did not say that it is not only women that have to consciously work for respect. Think of the different ethnic groups, religions, physical makeups, etc. Unfortunately humans impose this "respect earning pressure" on each other.

Are the factors that create respect at work the same factors as those that create respect at home?
Yes, basically, but some elements differ. I am "me" in both places and I'm consistent in both places. Even though there are always new elements being introduced, the rules for treating people fairly and respectfully never change.

My profession as a speaker, consultant, and personal computer applications trainer requires that I am thorough and that I express all answers in the language of my audience. Impressing them with my knowledge will not help them or me. (Laughing!)

As a result of this commitment to listen to their needs and to respond in a manner that is clear has been the biggest contributor to my success. Constantly I am referred to as "the most patient trainer" they have ever worked with.

What would you advise women to do to be taken seriously – by men and women?
First, be sure you are taking yourself seriously. Realize that you will have to consistently work at how people see you - and don't regret that requirement. Get yourself a plaque that says, "The Race Is Already Won!" Accept that it is won and that all you have to do is just keep running. Running with knowledge of victory just demands that you are taken seriously.

It's a beautiful thing to be a woman. Enjoy it, appreciate it and know that you are, and have always been, **powerful**. It has been the strength of the Black Woman throughout the years that has held her family unit together - especially in the tormenting days of slavery. However she is not alone. Ask the women of other cultures. To quote a line from *My Big Fat Greek Wedding*, "The man is the head, but the woman is the neck. Remember we turn the head." Accept the challenges - you're capable - then go for it!

Lorraine G. Stephens, www.lorrainestephens.com

Divorced. Two children. Son – Dorrian Kito Stephens (age 27). Daughter – Tiffany Siti Stephens (age 25). I was born December 30th .I am an only child born in Harlem (New York City). Grew up in Harlem and spent time with my grandparents in South Carolina.

PROFESSIONAL SUMMARY
A seasoned professional with thirty-three years of experience in management, consulting, course development, courseware and computer applications training, executive presentations, writing and speaking. A dependable, thorough and well-organized individual who communicates effectively, and has a flair for imaginative approaches to training.

ACCOMPLISHMENTS
As a consultant to one of the largest school districts in North Carolina, I provided the following services:

Central Office Staff - Designed and delivered applications training to over four hundred staff.

School Principals - Developed Laptop Training for the elementary, middle and high school principals.

Teachers - Delivered training to over two thousand teachers as they prepared to integrate technology into the classroom.

Developed/taught classes in: Microsoft Office, Using the Internet, Windows, Microsoft Publisher, LAN Concepts, FrontPage, Programming languages

EDUCATION: St. Augustine's College, Raleigh, North Carolina, BS Degree - Math and Physics, 1969 Graduate

HONORS AND ACHIEVEMENTS
Recognized by the Executive Women's Program Business Leader Component as one of "Today's Leaders"

Keynote speaker at the Carol Middle School Minority Achievement Reception

2002 Inductee into the YWCA Academy of Women – Science and Technology Division

2002 Women in Business inductee

Impact 100 Business leaders – 2003

2002 Friends of Justice recognition – North Carolina Justice and Community Development Center

Published, "I Wish I Had Known That Yesterday! – A friendly end user guide for accomplishing several tasks in Microsoft Word.

Co-authored *"Life, Work and Money From a Woman's Perspective"*

2002-2003 Woman of the Year - American Business Association - Raleigh Triangle Chapter

Mitzi Schaden Tessier

Do you generally feel respected as a woman?
Yes, especially by those younger than I am-- and most people are. (Laughing!)

What is your own personal definition of "respect"?
The feeling that a person is honorable and worthy of attention.

What did you do differently than most women to get where you are?
I had phenomenal luck. My first book, *Asheville, a Pictorial History,* was a gift from God. I met a representative from the publisher in an airport. Within a month I had a contract to do the book. Twenty thousand copies and twenty years later it went out of print. The second book, *The State of Buncombe,* written ten years later, is still selling.

Was respect something you had to consciously work to achieve?
The books made me a local "celebrity," particularly among younger adults. (Laughing!) I don't take my work seriously, so it's always a surprise and a delight to be treated with such respect.

Are the factors that create respect at work the same factors as those that create respect at home? Whoever gets respect at home? (Laughing) I'm just Mom! I think my kids and grandkids respect my judgment. They actually ask for my opinions, though we often differ. My "celebrity" status in the community sometimes rubs off on them. Though, on the

other hand, we are sometimes known as their parents because of their achievements.

What would you advise women to do to be taken seriously – by men and women?

♀ Try to know people for who they are. Then, you can talk to them about their interests.

♀ Don't force yourself into areas where you meet resistance. Have more respect for yourself than to go where you're not wanted.

You can be whatever you want to be, but don't try to be something you aren't.

Mitzi Schaden Tessier is an Oakie by birth, having first seen light of day in Supulpa, Oklahoma April 7, 1924. Greatest accomplishment: a happy marriage that has lasted 57 years, four successful, happy children, eleven grandchildren, and four great grandchildren.

Graduate of Louisiana State University with a BA in Journalism. Graduate work with University of North Carolina at Asheville and Western Carolina University.

Professional fields include teaching high school English and Special Education, Field Director for the Girl Scouts, and author of two pictorial histories: Asheville, a Pictorial History and The State of Buncombe.

Avocations: mission education and promotion, teaching the

history of our city to the College for Seniors and University Continuing Education classes, speaking to many groups about the history, and helping to place in our city a walking trail that tells the history of downtown Asheville.

"I'm willing to fall on my face
but not on my ass.
At least when you fall on your face,
you're moving forward."
Debra Winger, actress

Stephanie Volo

Do you generally feel respected as a woman?
I do!

What is your definition of "respect"?
You have to believe in yourself in enough to know that you're not better than others nor are they better than you; you're part of the team. Model loving, caring, and empowering others.

Respect is earned whether you are a man or a woman. You can't be chauvinistic. I treat others the way I want to be treated and try to make decisions for my team. I lead by example.

What did you do differently than most women to get where you are?
Not much. *But I have passion*! I was not a scholar, although I do believe in life education. I went to school for education and although I am not "teaching" I am learning and developing my team at all times. I have a positive attitude, and I believe that all things become learning experiences, if you look for the lesson.

Many entrepreneurs can't "let go" and as an owner, the most important thing is to know your limits and be able to empower those around you. When you know you need help – just ask.

Was respect something you had to consciously work to achieve?

I started at *The Gap* as a 20-year-old assistant manager and I wanted to be everybody's "friend." I quickly found out that respect was more important than having everyone like me.

Are the factors that create respect at work the same as those that create respect at home?
For me, yes. I try to be totally consistent in all my relationships. I talk with them, not at them, and I live by the Golden Rule; I try to treat others the way I wish to be treated. My teammates are my partners.

What would you advise women to do to be taken seriously – by men and women?
♀ Know that respect is always earned. Respect yourself and others are more likely to respect you.
♀ Be confident rather than thinking you know everything.
♀ Be yourself and know your own limits.

Empower your team.
Be willing to ask questions.

Stephanie Volo - President and Co-Owner, Planet Dog
Steph used to be a serious gymnast for 15 years. Some say, she looks just like Mary Lou Retton. She doesn't really love that but she certainly has her energy. Steph is a multi-tasking guru. She lives in Kennebunk, Maine with her husband Woody and best friend Chauncy, a chocolate lab. Born 8/18/69 in Sturbridge, MA and grew up in New Hampshire with one younger brother.

Professional Credentials – She started 1988 with the **Gap Corporation** and worked for them at **Gap, Gap Kids, Old Navy** divisions for 6 years – retail management, training, visual merchandising and store openings. Mostly traveled across the country to open stores and hire & train management teams. Volo then worked at **Natural Wonders** and **Warner Brothers Studio Stores Division** doing the same thing for both of those companies – including, multi store management. Strengths include strong management, communication & people development skills. She has spoken at many seminars on communication, people development, management and merchandising.

As Planet Dog's fearless leader, Stephanie manages across the company, but focuses heavily on operations, product development, merchandising and business development. Stephanie came to Planet Dog from Stonewall Kitchen, another successful Maine company. During her 3-year tenure, she grew Stonewall Kitchen's retail division from two to six stores and from fifteen to seventy-five employees and an annual 60% sales growth. Under her leadership at Planet Dog, the company has grown from 3 employees and 3 canine product testers to 11 of each. In 1999, Planet Dog offered 76 SKU's (product varieties) that were sold in 82 stores to 244 retail customers. Today, they offer over 842 SKU's which are available in over 2,000 stores worldwide and purchased directly by over 7,000 retail customers.

Fast Company Magazine's March, 2003 issue features Planet Dog™ (www.planetdog.com) as a "leader of the pack." The Portland-based manufacturer and retailer of unique and innovative products for dogs and their owners, has been selected by Fast Company Magazine and its readers as one of 50 champions of innovation in the Second Annual Fast 50 Global Readers' Challenge.

Fast Company Magazine editors, along with help from its readers, conducted a worldwide search for ordinary people doing extraordinary things: unsung heroes and rising stars such as senior executives, in-the-trenches team leaders, engineers, marketers, and other high-impact players from all kinds of backgrounds.

"A tree with strong roots
can withstand the most violent storm,
but a tree can't grow roots
just as the storm appears on the horizon."
---the Dalai Lama

Joyce Weiss

Do you generally feel respected as a woman?
Absolutely! That's why I get hired. My new professional motto is "Be Direct With Respect."

What is your definition of "respect"?
When you respect yourself you'll get what you deserve from others. Always communicate in a positive way that is respectful.

What did you do differently than most women to get where you are?
I turned most of the people in my life OFF! (Laughing!) My "friends" told me I couldn't do things, they said "don't." I ignored that advice. I knew I was going to make it and I couldn't listen to nay-sayers. I have aligned myself with those who believe in me, and I believe in them. I was willing to ask for help.

Was respect something you had to consciously work to achieve?
Oh my yes! I grew up in the '50s, in a loving, traditional home. I was respected as a person but I didn't believe in myself.

Are the factors that create respect at work the same as those that create respect at home?
I think so. You are who you are! Look at the patterns in your life. If you communicate well and are considerate at home, you probably communicate well and are considerate at work.

What would you advise women to do to be taken seriously – by men and women?
♀ Practice strength.
♀ Get coaching, counseling or mentoring from women you respect as role models.
♀ We all tend to take ourselves too seriously. It's important to have fun.

It's the fire inside you that generates respect.

Joyce Weiss: I received my masters degree in counseling from Oakland University in MI I attained my Certified Speaking Professional designation from *The National Speakers Association* in 1993.

There are more than 4,000 Corporate Speakers; there is only ONE Corporate Listener. Joyce Weiss understands that the unique challenges of any group must be uncovered and understood before their unique message can be created. Only then can a team be led toward improvement. By helping your people understand themselves and their passions, speaker and author Joyce Weiss helps them achieve their personal and professional bests. She then offers Bold Solutions to Boost the Bottom Line™ while improving their lives. **www.joyceweiss.com**

Live your life to the fullest, no matter what the terrain! In her new book, *Take the Ride of Your Life!* author/speaker Joyce

Weiss shows you how to use those bike-lesson memories to energize your self and your journey. Joyce has written over 50 articles for such publications as **USA Today, Cosmopolitan, Inc., Ladies Home Journal, Executive Excellence,** and **Personal Excellence,** to name but a few, and has another highly praised book, Full Speed Ahead: Become Driven by Change.

I was born 4/25/45 yet feel like I'm in my 40's. I have one sister, Marcia who lives in MI. Actually all my relatives live in MI! Lucky me! I was not always this bold and was shy as a little girl. This bold "stuff" started when I was in my 40's and it grows daily. I am the youngest sibling. My parents gave me the confidence that I have today and I think about how fortunate I have been compared to so many angry people who hate their past.

I have been married for 36 years to Jerry Weiss, an attorney. We enjoy bike riding. We have 2 married children and 3 grandchildren. We all live in Michigan. We live in West Bloomfield MI and I grew up in Oak Park,

As human beings,
our greatness lies not so much
in being able to remake the world...
as in being able to remake ourselves.
-- Mahatma Gandhi

Ann Westergaard

Do you generally feel respected as a woman?
Yes.

What is your own personal definition of "respect"?
I usually feel respected when I'm so comfortable with someone and keyed into his or her interests that I don't think about myself. As a Shaklee Distributor, if they don't "get it," I just haven't been able to communicate that I'm not "selling" but sharing what has really happened for me and that it can be for their advantage too if they want it.

What did you do differently than most women to get where you are?
I stuck with it. It took me a long time to make a serious commitment to my business but when I finally understood how I could make a worthy contribution, I became unstoppable. I do something EVERY day. My business fits into everything I do while I'm doing normal everyday things. Any time I got discouraged, I thought about the alternative: "A REAL JOB" without the freedom of choosing my own hours. A real job would probably pay me what I'm "worth" instead of this career I'm lucky enough to have which pays much more. (Laughing!)

I try to do at least two things a day that I'd rather not do (make phone calls, write a note, file, do a mailing, etc.) because the extra effort is what moves me forward. I can handle two things a day when the rest is just the fun of interacting with people.

My life has become so much better than it ever could have been with a traditional job. I advise people to describe the realities of a home-based business to their family, and request their support. You'll need to explain to your family that because there aren't set hours, as most jobs require, you will have more time to spend taking children to activities, etc. On the other hand, it will be necessary to spend some evenings and other times building the business. Ask: "Since this business is for our future. Will you help me?"

Was respect something you had to consciously work to achieve?
It is sometimes very difficult to get respect from your family. When you have a home-based business some people just tend to take you less seriously. In many minds it isn't a "real job." I've never quite understood why working at a regular job, which may not have an opportunity to grow, is looked at with more respect. That's just the way it is.

Are the factors that create respect at work the same factors as those that create respect at home?
Probably not. At work you have definite guidelines and a BOSS! How many people really feel respected at their job? (Laughing!)

What would you advise women to do to be taken seriously – by men and women?
♀ Succeed! Start making money and stick with it. When you have money you don't have to think about it.
♀ Invest in yourself to raise your self-esteem and get good at what you do
♀ Don't waste your life "getting ready" -- just do it now! Put blinders on and focus. Hang loose! Decide what's important and look at the big picture.

- ♀ Involve yourself with training that is offered. Interact and Question!
- ♀ Understand that we MAKE our own ENTHUSIASM! It doesn't just happen.
- ♀ Sometimes you'll not get respect and it doesn't matter.
- ♀ When you wake up in the morning Pretend to be Cheerful. By 10 a.m. you will be!

Money is a report card. If your bank account isn't growing, you're not doing enough to help others. Money should to be like a river. It ought to rush in -- and rush out!

Ann Westergaard: Married 47+ years, born March 2, 1935, in Des Moines, Iowa. As a child, lived in State College, Penn., and spent teen years in Buckland, Virginia. I have one younger brother.

Three years of college (Richmond Professional Institute in Richmond, Va. and Florida State) Parents were early environmentalists so I grew up with appreciation of the fragility of the earth. They were high achievers who believed in doing work that was fun. I learned from them that getting the job done well was more important than just filling an 8-hour workday. Often it can be done in much less time and leaves time to LIVE.

Held a variety of jobs from teen years: Waitress, Secretary, Dining Room Hostess, Chambermaid, World Book salesperson, clerk in book store, etc. Enjoyed civic work as a member and officer in Jr. Woman's Club.

Shaklee has a way of "Praising One To The Top" for accomplishing small steps. My current title is Key Coordinator, but it is a pleasure to consider myself a "Lifetime Member."

Turning Points In My Life:
Summer job at Eastover Resort, Lenox, Mass. Where I worked summers during college years. Learned valuable lessons by working with the public. Met my future husband there.

Marriage and birth of my three children. Our children are all successful in their own lives. My husband is a retired mortgage banker who enjoys playing golf. He also does all the cooking as well as taking care of the business records!

I have enjoyed being part of Shaklee for over 30 years. There is always something new to learn, whether it be Nutrition, Air Purification, Water Purification, Environmental Cleaners, Skin Care and Makeup, or Salesmanship, and Business Building.

I love to go for the "Carrots" – rather than the "Sticks" so Shaklee has sent my husband, three children (plus a son-in-law) and myself on many trips all over the world. (That's my HOT BUTTON) Also, since they give everyone an opportunity to earn "Bonus Cars" I am now driving my 10th. (A Lexus) I've especially loved having people in my organization earn trips, cars and cash too. My passion is teaching people to have healthier lives with interesting things to accomplish. I love helping Mom's who wish to stay home with their children, earn while they enjoy family life. Also, since I am married to a retired man, I love giving that (retired) age group new things to think about and so they will have many rewards to look forward to. (Note: I'm that age too, but I'll never retire!)

Anna Soo Wildermuth, AICI, CIP

Do you generally feel respected as a woman?
Yes, I think I am generally respected as a woman.

What is your definition of "respect"?
I've not been told that I'm too emotional, which is what men tend to say when they don't respect woman. When people value my opinions and my different perspective, I feel respected. I think my opinions have been appropriately considered and when they haven't been, it's not because I'm a woman.

What did you do differently than most women to get where you are?
I'm not very feminine in the sense that I don't giggle or make jokes. I'm not cutesy and I don't flirt. I'm very straightforward and direct. I think sometimes women do those traditionally feminine things and it hurts them professionally.

Was respect something you had to consciously work to achieve?
Others have always respected me, although I've always been aware that I had to work at it. I prepared myself by being knowledgeable, doing the right things, and I always try to see the bigger picture.

Are the factors that create respect at work the same as those that create respect at home?
Yes.

What would you advise women to do to be taken seriously – by men and women?

♀ Study role models.

♀ Understand different perspectives.

♀ Be clear about what you want and how you want to accomplish it.

♀ Don't worry about what others think and ignore others' criticism.

♀ Nurture other women.

Let things go. State facts, don't provide details until they are requested.

Anna S. Wildermuth, AICI, CIP owner of Personal Images, Inc. (**www.personalimagesinc.com**) is a recognized leader in the image industry, a seasoned professional image specialist, trainer and coach since 1983. She has been featured in Chicago Tribune, quoted as an expert in variety of local and national publications, Success, Chicago Magazine and featured on television programs including CNN-Financial, Fox News and published numerous articles in local and national publications and is the so co-author of *Unlocking the Secrets of Successful Women in Business.*

Anna is an active professional member of *Association of Image Consultants International* and in-coming President 2003-2005 and an Advanced Toastmaster. She is a board member of Chicago Minority Business Development Council, Inc., The Ray Graham Foundation for the Disabled Trustee and a member of American Society of Trainers and Development.

Anna has helped numerous Chicago and nation wide businesses and individuals make the critical first impression. Anna has helped executives and management teams of many large corporations strategize their professional image and understand the nuances of business/social etiquette and diversity. She understands that while the "uniform" created for an attorney, a Fortune 500 VP and a health care professional may have some common elements; they also have decided differences, which will enhance or minimize the wearer's credibility.

The President of **Personal Images, Inc.,** Anna founded her company in March of 1993. Individual clients include CEO's and executive directors, event planners, retirees, executive wives and for professionals preparing for television and platform appearances. Corporate clients include Schneider Electric-Square D Company, Sears Roebuck Company, Northern Trust Company and Household International. Anna's early career included sales success as a real estate broker, where she achieved lifetime membership in the Two Million Dollar Club.

Anna's civic involvement has included developing programs for Women Employed, Jane Addams Resource Corporation, and YWCA Target Program for Adults in Transition and Family Shelter For Abused Women in Stoney Island, Illinois.

Anna is divorced, the mother of one grown son, has a dog, and was born and raised in the Chicago area.

Nicole Williams

Do you generally feel respected as a woman?
Yes, I've never experienced a lack of male respect and have seldom ever felt disrespected.

What is your definition of "respect"?
Consideration, appreciation, setting boundaries and working around weaknesses. Respect is based on acceptance, good listening skills and bringing yourself fully to the table.

What did you do differently than most women to get where you are?
I was willing to endure discomforts. Success takes effort. Fear causes discomfort and success requires persistence. You have to go the extra mile, you have to face the fear, you have to go through the wall because it's infinitely easier on the other side. When you reflect back on your purpose and your commitment, you find the will to keep going.

I refused to be sucked into the negative feedback from others. I wouldn't be told what I could and couldn't do. I created my own standards for myself.

Was respect something you had to consciously work to achieve?
It never occurred to me. Respect, for me, includes creating my own boundaries I believe our feelings of self-respect are somewhat transparent. The more I respect myself the more I get it back from others.

Are the factors that create respect at work the same as those that create respect at home?

Oh, yes! At home I can be very honest with my husband, very direct without having to explain my frame of reference. The strategies are the same but the tactics are different

What would you advise women to do to be taken seriously – by men and women?

♀ You can't ask others to invest in you if you're not willing to invest in yourself.

♀ Don't wait until you feel "perfectly" prepared, skilled, ready – life will pass you by.

♀ Attitude is everything

♀ People respect people who respect themselves.

Think the unthinkable!

Nicole Williams – Co-Founder of *Wildly Sophisticated*!
I've been married for 3.5 years. No pets - would love them but we're too busy building our careers right now!! Born September 7, 1970 in Ajax, Ontario, Canada - suburb outside of Toronto. I have one brother who is just 16 months younger.

People come to Nicole for career advice, probably because she always has her stuff together. Along her quest, Nicole decided she should turn her natural "career advice" talents and interests into a business. To look at her resume, you would think Nicole strategically planned this career move, although she swears she didn't. Achievement highlights include: two university degrees (political science and social policy), studying women and work in Russia, acting as a national represen-

tative at APEC's Women Leaders Network in New Zealand, working as program coordinator for Career and Technology at the National Institute for the Blind, serving as federation chair for the University Women's Club and the list goes on.

Nicole recognizes that meaningful work is essential for creating life success – and she wants others to realize this, too. Nicole is working towards a goal or a purpose: watch out! You better be ready to join the fantastic ride or be prepared to get run over. She leads with unparalleled commitment, energy and vitality. When Nicole loves something she will make you love it, too. Visit **www.WildlySophisticated.com** and watch for Nicole's new book!

Life is a process of becoming,
a combination of states we have to go through.
Where people fail
is that they wish to elect a state
and remain in it.
This is a kind of death.
-Anais Nin

About the author:

Linda Brakeall, *The Respected Woman*, taught 5th grade at 19, was vice president of a national seminar company at 26, then spent 13 years in real estate as a high-producing salesperson, manager, corporate trainer and vice president. She opened Phoenix Seminars, headquartered near Chicago, IL, in 1992 and has produced sales-training, marketing and communication seminars all over America, specializing in the banking and mortgage industries. All this has established habits of success.

Linda says: "My strength lies not in teaching brand new information. Little exists that is truly new. My strength lies in connecting with people on their level and showing them how they can adapt this information and use it immediately to improve their personal and professional lives."

Linda Brakeall is the author of *The Respected Woman Series,* and co-author of *Unlocking The Secrets of Successful Women in Business* and the *Founder of The Respected Woman Month. (October)*

Nationally known as a sought-after media guest, dynamic keynote speaker, trainer, and seminar leader, Linda Brakeall is featured in the *National Speakers' Association's WHO'S WHO IN PROFESSIONAL SPEAKING* and takes "respect" to the next level for women and for corporations. *www.TheRespectedWoman.com.*

Your Notes, Observations, and AHA's!

Strength does not come from physical capacity.
It comes from an indomitable will.
-Mahatma Gandhi

Your Notes, Observations, and AHA's!

Difficult people are the greatest teachers.

- Pema Chodron

Your Notes, Observations, and AHA's!
There is no failure except in no longer trying.
-E. Hubbard

Your Notes, Observations, and AHA's!

Life can only be understood backwards; but it must be lived forwards.   - Søren Kirkegaard

Others will underestimate us,

for although we judge ourselves

by what we feel capable of doing,

others judge us only

by what we have already done.

Henry Wadsworth Longfellow

Are you reading someone else's copy?
Get one for you or a friend!

<u>Online</u>   **www.TheRespectedWoman.com**
<u>Fax</u> this form to   253-295-3753.
<u>Phone</u>:   800-662-7248 Have your credit card handy.
<u>Email</u> to: Orders@TheRespectedWoman.com
<u>Mail</u> with your check or credit card information to:
Hawthorne Press, 11 Arrow Wood, Suite 2D, Hawthorn Woods, IL 60047

Please send me _____ copies of
How To Get Men To Take You Seriously in Business and in Life!
@ $19.00 each plus $1 for S & H . (5 or more books? S & H is FREE!)

☐ Send information on volume discounts for fund-raisers or corporate sales.

☐ Please send FREE information on programs for in-house training,
    seminars, conferences, consulting, Respect-Able ™ Skill-Shops.

Name _____

Address _____

City, State, Zip _____

Telephone: (   ) _____

Email: _____

Sales Tax: Illinois residents, please add $1.33 per book.

Payment: Check enclosed for $_____
Charge my   Visa ____   Master Card ____

CC # _____

Exp. Date _____ Signature_____

Name on card: _____

<u>FREE Success articles.</u> **E-mail : Linda@TheRespectedWoman.com**